# D. H. LAWRENCE

# D. H. LAWRENCE

## ANTHONY WEST

**ARTHUR BARKER LIMITED**
20 NEW BOND STREET LONDON W 1

873 (Lawrence)
1HH x88
HBN

G20035111

Printed in Great Britain by
Lowe & Brydone (Printers) Ltd., London

## CHAPTER I

LAWRENCE has suffered, perhaps more than any other writer, from the devotion of his biographers. The normal way in which the ghost of a writer becomes transformed into a character in biography follows a stereotyped pattern. The man dies, and his widow, his heirs, or his literary executors, pay tribute to him in an official biography : this work of piety, and perhaps a few discreet personal memoirs, stands as an adequate record through the fifteen or twenty years of public indifference which always follows death. When, after that, the work shows its enduring power, curiosity kindles about the nature of the brain behind it, and biographers set to work to find the man behind the pious legend. By then, however, the real person has slipped away with his secrets ; time has eased resentments, and distresses, that might have given an edge to the tongues of those who were close to him, and they have had time to reject what was petty and unimportant in their relationships. None of this healing process took place before biographies of Lawrence began to appear. His anarchist side had destroyed the apparatus that might have produced an official biography, and the personal memoirs of his friends, being the raw stuff of resentment and distress, cannot be called discreet. Some of these memoirs appeared so soon after his death that it is possible to suspect that they had been, like newspaper obituaries, held in readiness for the event ; they were full of passion about the petty and the unimportant, and the impression they make is, inevitably, of a petty, trivial character.

Lawrence was one of those people with a rich emotional life who become emotional topers. He found friendship an inadequate relationship ; he had to go beyond it, to become a lover, to possess the whole mind. All through his life he played with the idea of *Rananim*—a community of those who had given up the world to go into a place apart, to live life as Lawrence believed it should be lived. He tested people by asking them to throw up everything for this community ; he was really asking for their complete devotion to himself. With one type of personality, possibly an immature type, acquaintanceship, friendship, love, are all reduced to a process of absorption, exhaustion and rejection. Lawrence turned his full powers on to anyone who attracted him, absorbed and captivated them, and then—just as soon as they were convinced that they had become the centre of his world—he moved on to some new emotional feeding-ground in a new person. It took a very level head to see that this process of absorption and rejection was natural to Lawrence, and the pain of it the natural penalty of coming anywhere near understanding him. Few of his friends were stout-hearted enough to bear it. As soon as Lawrence was dead there was a rush of wounded and abandoned people who were concerned to present to the world the picture of that golden period in which Lawrence found the centre of his being in them. They were also at pains to let the world know that the golden period ended through no defects of theirs, but because some third party maliciously intervened. Each writer was alone in understanding Lawrence, each was concerned to prove that he or she alone was capable of answering to Lawrence's burning spirit, all later relationships in Lawrence's life were necessarily fatal to his creative gift. The reader who attempts to approach Lawrence by way of these books gets the impression of little but the fierceness of the emotional competition which went on about him. The competition was fought without rules, and the energy with which the unsuccessful competitors defamed each other led them to extremities of libel. What they say about each other is disgusting, and the common reader can be pardoned for thinking that Lawrence himself was, as the centre of a disgusting set, a disgusting character.

When Mr. Hugh Kingsmill wrote his bitter attack on Lawrence in 1938, describing him as a hysteric with an eye to the main chance, or as a sexual incompetent with homosexual tendencies, it was unnecessary for him to go to any hard labour with the muck-rake. The work had already been done, and all Mr. Kingsmill had to do was to take scissors to books written by people who claimed to be Lawrence's friends. It was not necessary for him to put any gloss on their texts, or to do any interpretation; nothing could do Lawrence's reputation more harm than direct quotation. Lawrence, in the books of E. T., of Murry, Brett, Luhan and Carswell, is like the charm in the folk-tale that must be sold for a lower price each time it changes hands till it comes to be worth a grain of sand, a dead leaf, nothing. Lawrence made an irritated comment on this process of devaluation when he saw it launched with the publication of Aldous Huxley's *Point Counter Point*, in which he figures as Rampion; when the book was published he wrote a letter to Huxley, saying :

> your Rampion is the most boring character in the book—a gas bag. Your attempt at intellectual sympathy ! It's all rather disgusting, and I feel like a badger that has its hole on Wimbledon Common and trying not to be caught.

One immediate reaction to this is sympathetic—but then—

Lawrence was himself guilty of quarrying gossip about his friends for material ; he always made the heaviest possible demands for intellectual sympathy ; and if he resented being caught why did he do so much catching ? Like all extreme romantics, like all people who live at the beck and call of emotion, Lawrence's personal life is a kaleidoscopic pattern of light and shadow, calm and storm—a jolt and its mood abruptly changes from joy to despair—like any other manifestation of disorder it must inevitably be detestable to those who have, or like, the classical temper.

Lawrence was born in a little house, a small shop and upper part, in Victoria Street, Eastwood, in the Nottingham coalfield, on 11th September 1885. A small shopkeeper can at least flatter himself that he is in business on his own account, that he is an independent business man, and it was probably this motive which led Lydia Lawrence into the business of selling lace caps, aprons and linen. She was trying to keep the status she had lost with her marriage. Her father was an engineer in the Sheerness dockyard, a black-coat worker who had taken trouble with her education. She was at one time a school teacher, she read novels and poetry, she spoke the refined, unlocal language of the urban middle class. When she was twenty or thereabouts— assuming that Mrs. Morel of Lawrence's *Sons and Lovers* is a portrait of Lydia Lawrence, and that the portrait is substantially correct—she became attached to a young man of the same class, also a teacher. She imagined that he was as much in love with her as she with him, and it was something of a shock when he went off and married a widow with property. When she was still under the influence of the shock she met and married a well-set-up, handsome

man, a gay singer, reputed to be the best dancer in his
district : a great laughing, jolly fellow with a full luxuriant
beard. She thought that he owned his house, and that he
had substantial savings, but he was in fact living from one
week's pay to the next on his earnings as an underground
worker in a coal pit. He was not a property owner, he
was a manual labourer, a member of the working classes,
and according to her standards she had married, disastrously,
beneath her.

As time went on, and five children were added to the
family, the horrors of the mesalliance increased for Lydia.
Her husband assumed that the children were of his own
class. Like him they would speak book English on grand
occasions and drop into the easy local dialect when talking
among themselves ; when they grew up the boys would go
down the pit, and the girls would go into domestic service.
Lydia Lawrence, however, was not going to put up with
this : she might have touched pitch and been defiled, but
her children were not going to pay any penalty for her
error. She brought the children up never to speak their
father's low-class language within earshot of her, and to
despise all those who lived—as their father did—by manual
labour. Everything specifically working class was anathema ;
in effect the father was frozen out of the household, his place
in it was that of a lodger who paid the household bills.

This situation had been deteriorating for ten years when
Lawrence was born ; by the time he was able to take notice
all attempt to make anything of the marriage had been
abandoned. The father and mother were getting their
interest in life out of their successes in the unending
war between them. She would establish scores by lifting
the conversation over his head into the realms of poetry,

literature and religion ; he would establish counter-scores by coarse dialect interjections thrust into the high-toned conversation of such desirable visitors as the Congregational Minister—if these reduced the visitors to embarrassed silence or drove them from the house so much the better. Then there were battles between her tongue and his silence ; he would try to sulk out her scoldings, she would try to goad him into an outburst of temper or into leaving the house. Eastwood, like other British industrial villages, had at that time only one social focus apart from the home and the church or chapel—the public-house. When Lydia Lawrence scolded her husband out of the house that was the only place he could go to, and there was nothing surprising in his taking a jar when he got there. Mrs. Lawrence was a teetotaller of a fanatic type, so that if her husband came home with his breath scented by three or four pints he was a drunken brute staggering home stinking of drink. He would come home in a glow, with his rage eased and full of good humour, a little apologetic about the ill-temper in which he had gone out : she, having spent the time feeding up her sense of grievance, would be waiting for him with several mouthfuls of venom. She would nag, nag, nag at him until he was turned into a shouting, raging beast. The children lay upstairs, listening.

There were five children ; George, Ernest, Emily, Herbert and Ada. George inherited his father's physical grace and good looks, but he was not clever at winning certificates and diplomas. Lydia scored a dubious success in the business of lifting him out of the working class right away. He was apprenticed to an uncle, a picture-framer in Nottingham ; all that can be said is that he got away from Eastwood and the pit. The second son—Ernest—was an unqualified success from the start; he left school armed with a bundle of certificates and immediately showed his superiority to father by getting a job as a clerk in a local colliery office, and later with the Co-operative Society. Working hard on correspondence courses and at night school he learned typewriting, shorthand, French and German. Thus armed he went off to glory, the shipping office of a London firm. From glory he came back to take holidays in Eastwood, gloriously dressed in topper, frock-coat, stiff white collar, and neat grey choker. His family looked at him with awe, and Eastwood with envious amazement.

He was held up to Herbert as an example; and Herbert settled down to beat him at the same game. He collected certificates and diplomas even more rapidly, and at sixteen was ready to escape into the respectable commercial world. He turned to Ernest for advice on the first necessary step towards getting a clerkship, and together they wrote a letter to a Nottingham firm of surgical goods manufacturers:

GENTLEMEN,—In reply to your ad. in to-day's G.* for a Junior Clerk, I beg to place my services at your disposal. I am sixteen years of age, and have just completed three years' course at the Nottingham High School. Although I have not had any business experience in accounts yet, I studied book-keeping and obtained two prizes for mathematics, as well as one for French and German.

If desired, I shall be pleased to furnish you with the highest references as to character and ability, both from my late masters and the minister in this town.

Should you favour me with the appointment I would always endeavour to merit the confidence you place in me. Trusting to receive your favourable reply,—I beg to remain, gentlemen, Yours obediently,—D. H. LAWRENCE.

He was favoured with the appointment, and so, like

* " to-day's G."—the *Nottingham Guardian*.

H. G. Wells in the draper's shop, made a false start in life :
like Wells he realised it, and went back to make another
start. After a year in the office he went back to Eastwood
to take a post as pupil teacher in the British school and was
out of the business trap, again on the course followed by
Wells. As a pupil teacher he had opportunity to study—
and even if the aim was still the narrow one of qualifying
as a teacher, wider horizons began to come into sight. The
teacher's training was a much more liberal education than
the clerk's training he had been getting, and Lawrence's
reading began to enlarge rapidly in scope, to embrace almost
everything in print between Euripides and the novels of
Meredith. French and German, too, became more than
part of the necessary equipment of a shipping clerk, and he
began to be aware of richer, alien worlds than the one his
mother knew, and in which she intended him to cut a
successful figure. In the actual business of training as a
teacher Lawrence was apt and quick : he went from the
British school at Eastwood to a training centre for un-
certificated teachers at Ilkeston, and from that place to
Nottingham University College, where he spent two years—
from the time he was eighteen until he was twenty. Then
as a fully qualified teacher he went off to London, to a post
in the Davidson Road Schools at Croydon.

Inevitably this use of the free educational machinery added
to the normal difficulties of Lawrence's adolescence and
early manhood. A Trades Union leader, a Clydesider, once
raised bitter objection to that machinery on the ground that
it did not lead to the improvement of the working class,
but led to its impoverishment : he said that it skimmed the
cream off the working class and enlisted its best young
people in the ranks of the bourgeoisie. For all that it is in

the devitalised language of politics there is a good deal of truth in the remark : it looks as if it were a Marxist reach-me-down, but it is in fact based on knowledge of the personal suffering which is the lot of those who follow Lawrence's path. When he was sixteen Lawrence could write the letter, applying for the Nottingham post, without doubt, either about the letter itself, or about the quality of mind which led his brother Ernest to approve it. He then almost certainly admired Ernest as much as the other members of the family did, and admired his refinement as much as he despised his hard-handed father's coarseness. " I'm a man and I'll do man's work if tha'lt treat me right," was his father's lumpy independent attitude. Lawrence had been tricked by his mother, and Ernest, into believing that it was a finer thing to say that *should you favour me with the appointment I would always endeavour to merit the confidence you place in me*, and generally, to crawl. In his education Lawrence came to know the aristocratic mind of the creative writer, which is humble in a way which has nothing to do with *furnishing references, if desired*. Lawrence was writing his first poems soon after he was sixteen, and he had a novel completed by the time he was twenty : his mind was not only expanding rapidly, but he was also becoming aware of the abnormal creative gift he possessed, that he was of the company of Whitman, Blake, Euripides. The more he became aware of the standards they are judged by, and by which he was to be judged if he were to be of their company in more than promise, the more, then, he became aware of the pettiness of the standards which made Ernest's achieve-ments admirable. It would have been easy enough for Lawrence to despise his brother's standards, and to pass on to other things : but the driving force behind his brother was his mother—and, although it was easy enough to despise his father in alliance with her, it was difficult to despise either without any supporting alliance of blood. Even the most rebellious of children usually take the side of one parent against the other to win sanction for their outbreak.

The death of Ernest added enormously to the difficulty of this situation : he died with shattering abruptness in London and was beyond aid or recognition by the time that his family reached his bedside. He had not had time to achieve anything like the success that his mother had planned for him, and the whole burden was transferred to Lawrence's shoulders : he was to succeed for her. Then, just as Lawrence was nerving himself to declare that his purpose in life was writing, art, and not material success, a further psychological complication was added—Lydia Lawrence began to die of cancer. The unconscious mind works in such a way that it is probable that in Lawrence's case the conscious desire to repudiate what his mother stood for was translated by his unconscious mind into a desire to be rid of her altogether. The unconscious mind is beyond the pale of reason, by definition, and subject of delusions, one of which is that a wish will kill : this delusion endlessly puts it in the position of Henry after the murder of Thomas à Becket, saddled with real guilt by a word heedlessly uttered from the conscious forepart of the mind. Paul Morel, the hero of *Sons and Lovers*, is to some extent a self-portrait, and his adventures and sufferings are based largely on Lawrence's real and phantasy lives ; the truth of the novel's account of his mother's death, and of the illness leading up to it, is confirmed by Ada Lawrence in her memoir of Lawrence's youth, and in the memoir by E. T. (who figures in the novel as Miriam). Neither, however, pays any attention to the significant detail in the novel—that Paul Morel kills his mother with an overdose of morphia and thinks of hastening the work of the drug by smothering her. While Lydia Lawrence was dying of cancer, Lawrence was finishing his first novel, *The White Peacock*, and a special printing was made so that she could read it before she died. But it was too late to convince her and prove to her that he was not being disloyal in deserting her safe respectable world. When she was dead the burden of guilt for her death settled on him; it was attached in particular to his activity as a novelist, as his essay on "The Novel," in *Reflections on the Death of a Porcupine*, shows clearly enough. But the feeling of guilt, of wrong-doing, embraced all his activity as a writer from the time of his mother's death : by an unhappy accident Lawrence as a writer was deprived at the outset of his career of the certainty in the value of creative art which is part of the creative artist's life blood.

In his escape from the Eastwood setting Lawrence had to break with associations he had made for himself as well as those he was born to. He had a friend, the daughter of a smallholder. She was much in love with him and she hoped to marry him (it was the girl who later wrote her own memoir of Lawrence under the initials E. T.). The book is an important contribution to the Lawrence myth, and Kingsmill makes full use of it in demonstrating that Lawrence was a mother-sick egotist consumed by the death-wish. But the memoir gives an account of Lawrence's adolescence which shows him, at sixteen, dominated by all the ideas which were developed in his books long after he had escaped Eastwood—it shows no trace of the Lawrence who could write as he wrote to the Nottingham manufacturer, and few traces of the ruthless self-improver lifting himself out of Eastwood by his own bootstraps who must have rapidly taken the place of the junior clerk. Perhaps because the differences between these callow figures and the later Lawrence explain, better than mother-sickness, and better than the death-wish, why little came of the early love.

It was, to tell the truth, unlikely to come to anything— even if Lawrence had not been a genius—because it began with pity. It was one of Lydia Lawrence's less endearing habits that she was a teller of hard-luck stories. She used to buttonhole the more prosperous members of the Congregational Chapel after service in order to walk home with them pouring out the story of the ill-treatment and ill-usage she suffered from her drunken husband. She collected E. T.'s mother in his fashion, and received a pitiful friendship as a sort of alms. Lydia used to take her children over to the farm worked by E. T.'s parents to be patronised, *poor things*. It would have been impossible for Lawrence to find anything attractive at the farm had not E. T. been, herself, in rather pitiable case—she had been withdrawn from school to act as unpaid housemaid at home and was fighting a hard battle to get back to school. Lawrence sympathised with her while the fight was going on ; and when it was won, and she was back at school training to be a teacher, they were covering the same ground, working ont he same text-books and required reading. Naturally Lawrence made her a friend, as naturally she took friendship for love. The misunderstanding could, no doubt, have continued indefinitely if they had remained fifteen and sixteen, but they became rapidly enough nineteen and twenty : then neighbours and relatives began to ask if they were courting. Lawrence suddenly realised the existence of the misunderstanding, and after explaining the difference between love and friendship, suggested that the friendship should continue without complication. E. T.'s reaction was violent, by her own account, and Lawrence was thrown into considerable confusion at finding himself, emotionally at any rate, very much in the wrong—without knowing it he had trifled with her affections. She wanted love and marriage, a dear little home, and dear little babies—and could see no reason why Lawrence shouldn't have the same healthy instinctive wishes. But for him marriage meant doubling the chances against getting out of Eastwood, and it also meant a state of squalid bondage—the beastly thing in which his parents were entrapped—and as a still unqualified teacher he was also aware that it must be several years before his professional earnings reached more than £100 a year. Common sense, experience and prudence all combined to warn him that it would be fatal to mortgage his future to the gold promise of calf love. And, moreover, as he told E. T., she was not physically attractive to him, and in his view no amount of sympathy, spiritual affinity or friendship could make a marriage if there were no healthy animal side to it. It was possibly a mistake to be as frank as that; it was certainly a mistake to tell her that physical attraction—without intellectual sympathy—would, on the other hand, be enough, and that he was thinking of marrying a good-looking local noodle who had—apparently—permitted him a few appetising liberties. Hurt, jealous, and outraged by his insistence on the importance of sex in human relationships, she conceived for her comfort the idea that there was something badly wrong with Lawrence; at the same time she fought to keep him by increasing her part in his intellectual life. Her determination to hang on was increased when the noodle proved to be unsatisfactory as a

companion, and her doggedness manifestly rattled Lawrence
badly. When he went off to take up his Croydon post
the situation between them was still unresolved : he still felt
the need of her intellectual companionship, he wanted to
discuss the ideas that struck him in other people's work with
her, and he wanted to offer his own work to her for
criticism. But physically, though she had made it plain he
was practically under an obligation to be attracted, he was
not drawn to her. He might have simply and easily out-
grown this affair as he found new intellectual interests in
London, but for the fact that these new intellectual interests
were found for him—and with them his career as a literary
man—by E. T. In the spring of 1908 Lawrence told E. T.
he was very discouraged because a parcel of his manuscripts
had been returned, apparently unread, by an author he
admired enough to ask for criticism. In December that
year Lawrence came up to Eastwood on his first holiday
from his post at Croydon, bringing with him a copy of
Ford Madox Hueffer's new magazine, the *English Review*.
The paper attracted E. T. and her family, and they took out
a subscription ; at the end of a few months E. T. was
convinced that the paper would be interested in Lawrence's
work, and, with his permission, she sent a number of his
poems to the editor. Hueffer was excited by them and
asked Lawrence to come and see him to discuss any other
work he might have done ; when this proved to be *The
White Peacock* he became really enthusiastic—he had discovered a genius. He gave Lawrence a warm letter
recommending him to Heinemann, the publishers, and
began to ask him to the house. Heinemann took the novel
and the people at Hueffer's lunches took him seriously as
a promising and curious-minded young writer. Lawrence

ceased to be odd man out in Eastwood and began to change into a London success—and the change was, inescapably, due to that happy idea of E. T.'s.

Lawrence felt the obligation lying heavily on him. Soon after he'd begun work at Croydon he'd drifted, much to E. T.'s distress, into an engagement with an auburn-haired fellow-teacher. Now he wrote to E. T. saying that he had broken with this other woman, that he realised the mistake he had been making for so long, and that they ought now to consider themselves engaged. E. T. entered on a brief period of happiness which lasted through the spring of the year while he was working on the final revision of *The White Peacock*. But while he was still working at that he began to churn out *The Trespasser*—finishing it in just over three months, and working himself into a great state of emotional tension. E. T. was suddenly told that she was, after all, inadequate, there was a girl called Helen who was essential to him in some way and he must be free to have from both what they had to give. This was quite unacceptable to E. T., and the situation between them reverted to the familiar deadlock. At the beginning of August their engagement was broken off, the rupture coming a few days before Lawrence learned that his mother was about to die. Her illness was painful, and her long death agonising for her children; under its stress Lawrence entered on yet another engagement—breaking the news of it to E. T. with the serene brutality of the true egotist :

> I was in the train with X on Saturday and I suddenly asked her to marry me. I never meant to. But she accepted me and I shall stick to it—I've written to her father. . . . I'll go over the old ground again, if you like, and explain. Do you want me to say little, or nothing, or much ? I'll say anything you like, only I can't help it, I'm made this way.

Nevertheless when Lydia Lawrence died a fortnight later it was to E. T. that Lawrence immediately turned ; he spent the day before the funeral walking with her, talking about his own complex emotional condition, and about the ethics of the new engagement.

The engagement with X was broken off in February of 1911, after lasting for some seven months, apparently receiving its death-blow during the writing of *Sons and Lovers*. This novel was begun in 1910, when about an eighth part of it was put down on paper, and brought to the state of being some two-thirds complete in October of the following year. It was then a somewhat sentimental affair called *Paul Morel*, and E. T. thought it poor, unrealistic stuff when it was shown her for criticism. She had a clear mental picture of a battle between herself and Lydia for Lawrence's mental health and manly virtue ; she wanted it put in the book, which held all the other elements of the situation clearly enough, so she urged Lawrence to rewrite it—on the foundation of the truth. He saw that the novel would gain from being lifted to the level of intensity of their relationship, and in a bout of creative violence rewrote it in six weeks. It was the end of all attempt to maintain love or friendship between them—E. T. was scalded by the new picture of the central events of her life. She had not realised that if there is an absolute truth in philosophy there is not such a thing in psychology, where the truth is what you happen to believe ; still less did she realise the nature of the creative artist's split personality. Her own truth about herself and Lawrence differed so entirely from what was apparently Lawrence's vision of the same thing that she could not think about it at all—hurt beyond all bearing she didn't know how to bear it—without anæsthesia.

I tried hard to remind myself that after all *Sons and Lovers* was only a novel. It was not the truth, although it must inevitably stand for the truth. I could hear in advance Lawrence's protesting voice : " Of course it isn't the truth. It isn't meant for the truth. It's an adaptation from life, as all art must be. It isn't what I think of you, you know it isn't. What shall I put, what do you want me to put . . . ? " in a mounting crescendo of irritation and helplessness. I felt that words could only exacerbate the situation. The remedy must be left to time. And as I sat and looked at the subtle distortion of what had been the deepest values of my life, the one gleam of light was the realisation that Lawrence had overstated his case ; that some day his epic of maternal love and filial devotion would be viewed from another angle, that of his own final despair.

This was undoubtedly written in a spirit of complete sincerity, but however well it shows the way in which E. T. found consolation, it tells one nothing whatever about Lawrence. It is typical of the entirely egocentric character of E. T.'s memoir that she writes of her last, accidental meeting with Lawrence as if it was the end of his life, rounding off the account with a solemn remark, let fall by Lawrence's sister Emily : " Our Bert can never love any woman. He could only love his mother." An invocation which, however effective in the world of phantasy, fails to conjure Frieda Lawrence out of the real world.

## CHAPTER II

IN September 1911, when Lawrence reached the age of twenty-six, his life was turned in a new direction. Early in the year Heinemann published *The White Peacock*, *The Trespasser* and *Sons and Lovers* only needed a final revision before publication, Martin Secker had written offering to publish a volume of short stories, Ford Madox Hueffer's friends had given him a good critical send off, and Edward Garnett (acting as his agent out of sheer goodness of heart) was telling him that he could almost certainly find a publisher for anything he might write. Lawrence's professional career as a school teacher was beginning to cramp his professional career as a writer, and the strain of attempting to deal with both was undermining his health. He had already had several severe attacks of pneumonia in his childhood and adolescence to warn him that he was delicate ; the first, graver, warning signs of tuberculosis now appeared in the severest attack of all and it became obvious that he would have to take more care of himself. He decided, inevitably, that the schoolmastering must go, and accordingly applied for long leave of absence from the Davidson Road Schools. He did not throw up the job, but left it open in case he should fail as a writer : a prudent step characteristic of a side of Lawrence generally neglected by those who have written about him.

The winter passed slowly and drably. After a long struggle Lawrence shook off his illness at the end of December, and went to enjoy his convalescence in a Bournemouth boarding-house. In a month of vile weather he

revised *The Trespasser* which Edward Garnett had placed
with Duckworths. As he worked he decided he must get
out of England, give himself a change that would give him
a chance to get well ; he reckoned that he had just enough
money to do it by himself—if all went well—but he had
no margin of safety if he became ill again. It occurred to
him that he would have that if he could get a post as lecturer
at a foreign university, and in April 1912 he went to canvass
the possibilities of this idea with the man who had been his
instructor in French at Nottingham University, Professor
Weekley. On the seventeenth of that month he wrote a
happy, grateful, excited letter to Edward Garnett. He was
grateful because Garnett had arranged that one of his three
plays should be given a trial, wonderfully excited by Frieda
Weekley.

> I shall be in London next week, I think—from Thursday to
> Sunday—then I can see Walter De la Mare, and Harrison, who
> want to jaw me, and you who don't want to jaw me. Mrs.
> Weekley will be in town also. She is ripping—she's the finest
> woman I've ever met—you must above all things meet her . . .
> she's the daughter of Baron von Richthofen, of the ancient and
> famous house of Richthofen—but she's splendid, she is really.
> How damnably I mix things up. Mrs. Weekley is perfectly
> unconventional, but really good—in the best sense. I'll bet you
> never met anybody like her, by a long chalk. You must see
> her next week. I wonder if she'd come to the Cearne, if you
> asked us. Oh, but she is the woman of a life time.

The probabilities are very heavily against a man's meeting
a woman like Frieda Lawrence, even once in a lifetime. All
the men and women Lawrence had met so far lived in two
worlds—the world of ideas and belief, on the one hand, which
they inhabited in their dreams, and the world of necessities
and conventions in which they actually lived. Frieda
Lawrence recognised no such separation ; her marriage had

failed and she had decided that she must abandon the world
of necessity and convention for the world of ideas and belief
if she was ever to know happiness again. Lawrence was at
a stage of his development in which he was deciding that
ideas were meaningless divorced from action and nerving
himself to break with the world of necessity and convention ;
it is at least a possibility that without Frieda he would never
have made the break. It is probable that his many references
to his dependence on her relate to that possibility, and very
improbable that, as his detractors suggest, he simply found
in her a substitute for his domineering wasp of a mother.

It would be difficult to find two women resembling each
other less. Lydia Lawrence had a physique indelibly marked
by poverty, her mean features and poor bone structure
attesting to poor feeding throughout youth and adolescence,
her thin hair and bad teeth speaking just as clearly of lack
of proper care during or after her pregnancies ; psycho-
logically she was a weak character, a whiner and complainer,
one of the perpetually ill-used who trade on their weakness.
Frieda, on the other hand, in spite of having borne three
children, was in her splendid physical prime when Lawrence
first met her : she had been properly looked after all her life,
excellently fed, properly rested whenever fatigue or illness
threatened her. With her fine physique went a free and
independent mind ; she had a strong character armed with
a fierce pride, and the whining and complaining which goes
with an accepted inferiority was utterly foreign to her. Lydia
Lawrence put up with her extremely bad marriage, Frieda
broke her first marriage because it wasn't perfect—they were
as utterly different in their habits of mind as in physique.

The neurotic who is looking for a mother substitute may
look for something else than a simulacrum, may be looking

merely for a functional substitute, to cook, sew, mind the accounts, keep the home snug and warm, and provide a snug harbour from responsibility. When Lawrence met Frieda she was enormously incompetent from the domestic point of view: she records Lawrence's disgust when he found that she barely knew how to make a cup of tea, she had never done anything for herself of the practical kind, and it fell to Lawrence to teach her how to be independent and free of servants in everyday things. And, if she could not relieve him of any practical responsibilities, she could still less relieve him of any moral responsibilities—if he turned to her for reassurance in moments of doubt or weakness, deadly questions immediately began to formulate themselves ; he had to justify her ruthlessness in being untrue to her husband, her children and her blood. If Lawrence had proved weak and unimportant she would have been simply one adulteress among many ; she would also have joined the ranks of those with low tastes—the women of great houses who have gone off with hostlers, bootboys and footmen. Lawrence had to be strong and upright, or he would have betrayed Frieda most cruelly: the mother-and-son, protector-and-dependent relationship was quite impossible for them.

The relationship which did exist between them was a natural and extremely healthy one. When they first met she was thirty-one and he was twenty-six ; they were both mature physically and mentally, both ready for the best sort of marriage—an equal partnership which enriched them both. The five years between them did not amount to much to start with, and counted for less each year afterwards. It was not at any time a source of trouble between them, their often violent conflicts sprang from the pride they took

in each other. Whenever Lawrence saw Frieda declining
from her potential natural best into the stock patrician
attitudes of her upbringing he challenged her with a violent
attack ; and whenever she saw Lawrence compromising or
betraying his ideas with inconsistencies she challenged him.
As she had a considerable natural nobility, and as he was,
on the other hand, volatile and as unstable as water, she was
more frequently on the attack than he was, and more
successful in attack because he felt guilty about his inconsistencies—his mind was too acute for easy self-deceptions.
The important thing is, that their disputes were not the
normal symptoms of a failing, disintegrating marriage, but
were the natural price that perfectionists have to pay when
they marry, and signs of the reality of their partnership.

But all the same the affronted *manes* of the Weekley
household had to be pacified, and the hurt done to the
father and the children paid for. Ruthlessness in personal
relationships is its own reward. Lawrence and Frieda bolted
from England six weeks after they first met, and they were
still in flight when Lawrence died. Indeed, the flight continued after Lawrence's death, and his body was torn up
out of the graveyard at Vence long after he had abandoned
it, to be taken across the heaving seas to another resting-
place at Taos in Mexico. From the time of his elopement
Lawrence never belonged to any place, never was part of
any community ; he was a rootless wanderer in Bohemia,
and however hard he tried to merge himself into a place
and its life he remained an outsider who would be off again
when the wind blew in another quarter.

They stole away out of England on 3rd May 1912 and
went over the sea into Germany, into Frieda's world. They
arrived in the fortress town of Metz as Baron von Richthofen

was celebrating his fifty years of service with the Imperial Army, with a blaring of brass bands and a great concourse of well-born relatives. Frieda hadn't cleared herself altogether with Weekley, who only knew she'd gone, not that she'd gone with a man ; and the family in Metz didn't know that Lawrence was in their town. Breaking out and breaking in was a wearing, anxious business, and Lawrence was made to feel every inferior inch the miner's son while the Baron and Baronin met him and tested him to see if he was worthy of their daughter. After a few days Lawrence cleared out and went down the Rhine valley, first to Trier and then to Waldbrol, to wait rather wretchedly for a fortnight while Frieda fought herself clear of her family and her husband. She joined him at Munich at the end of the month, and after a week in a hotel at Beuerberg they moved to a flat in a house at Icking, the next village along the Isar valley, lent them by Professor Weber of Heidelberg University. The splendid happiness they knew here, as Frieda learned the hard business of living on fifteen shillings a week, and Lawrence learned about marriage, is described beautifully both in Lawrence's letters, and in Frieda's book *Not I but the Wind*—it is perhaps less satisfactorily described in the group of poems written at this time which Lawrence later published as *Look! We Have Come Through!* These raw expressionist poems are unpleasing at first reading because they go directly to matters which people, as a rule, manage to avoid facing although creative artists invariably deal with them. Catullus' poem, *Odi et Amo*, and the Shakespeare Sonnets, are very much about the way snakes live in rose beds : Frieda had just plunged into the new field of Freudian psychology when she met Lawrence, and she excited him about the theory of it—as an artist he recognised a new line of attack on this question of ambivalence—of loving mixed up with hating—and plunged in. He made the serpents intertwined with his roses so vividly alive for other people that their pretences about their own guaranteed-snake-free blossoms were endangered, and they resented it very much. There is nothing more repulsive to the habitually dishonest than honesty, and wandering through the flower-starred alpine pastures by the Isar Lawrence committed himself to honesty. It was inevitably a painful process, and the poems are not, as the letters were intended to be, light, amusing reading ; and Frieda's recollections are a distillation of the painful process.

Early in August they began to move south, first walking down the Isar valley to Mayerhofen in the Austrian Tyrol, some ten miles from Innsbruck ; and then after a fortnight or so, with David Garnett in their company, over the Brenner Pass by way of Sterzing and the Pfitzer Joch to Riva by Lake Garda. They'd started the move south with £23 in hand, and the position was fairly tight when they settled into the Villa Leonardi at Riva towards the end of the first week in September : and although an advance of £50 from Duckworths reached them there, they still felt that half a crown a day was more than they could afford for their room, and they moved down the lake shore and across the Austro-Italian frontier to Gargnano.

> They have to let, furnished, the bottom flat of the Villa Igéa—dining-room, kitchen, two bedrooms, furnished—big pretty rooms looking over the road on to the lake—a nice garden with peaches and bamboos—not big—for eighty lire a month—about 66s. a month—everything supplied. . . .

Here Lawrence settled down to hard work on his books, and on his ideas.

Before the end of the year *Sons and Lovers* was finally revised for publication (and a certain amount of Freudian theory written into it in the process). By the following April, when they left Gargnano, *Sons and Lovers* had been corrected in proof, two other novels were begun and taken beyond their first hundred pages, the sketches later published together under the title of *Twilight in Italy* roughed out, and several short stories written. But, if it was a highly profitable period from the point of view of work, Lawrence and Frieda were unprofitably isolated in this Italian village ; they had occasional visitors but they were not enough to break the circuit of ideas—out of Lawrence, through Frieda, back to Lawrence, out of Lawrence, through Frieda . . . round and round. There was no effective challenge from outside that might have forced Lawrence to accept some form of mental discipline. In January Lawrence wrote a letter to Ernest Collings which shows the direction his thought was taking ; after making several guesses at what personal troubles could be making Collings such an ineffective artist, Lawrence plunged :

> My own great religion is a belief in the blood, the flesh, as being wiser than the intellect. We can go wrong in our minds. But what our blood feels and believes and says, is always true. The intellect is only a bit and bridle. What do I care about knowledge. All I want is to answer to my blood, direct, without fribbling intervention of mind, or moral, or what not. I conceive a man's body as a kind of flame, like a candle flame, forever upright and yet flowing ; and the intellect is just the light that is shed on to the things around. And I am not so much concerned with the things around—which is really mind—but with the mystery of the flame forever flowing, coming god knows how from practically nowhere, and being itself, whatever there is around it—that it lights up.

A few days later Edward Garnett, who had had a postcard

telling him he might expect a foreword to *Sons and Lovers*
that would amuse him, was, one imagines, startled by a long
sermon in camp-meeting style :

> John, the beloved disciple says " The word was made flesh."
> But why should he turn things round ?  The women simply
> go on bearing talkative sons, as an answer.  " The Flesh was
> made word."  For what was Christ . . . ?

Edward Garnett, not having been told, like Collings, of
Lawrence's new purpose, cannot have followed the direction
and intention of the argument, and in any case can hardly
have been amused by it.

> . . . He was the word . . . and the word is not spoken by
> the Father, who is flesh for ever unquestioned and unanswerable,
> but by the Son.  Adam was the first Christ . . . and God the
> Father, the Inscrutable, the Unknowable, we know in the
> Flesh, in Woman.  She is the door of our in-going and our
> out-coming.  In her we go back to the father—but like the
> witnesses of the transfiguration, blind and unconscious. . . .

This is a whispering gallery in which there are many echoes,
of the near biblical language of the preachers in chapel, of
Rosicrucian doctrines, even of the early Christian Ophite
heresy (from which is drawn the light-and-flame image of
the letter to Collings, and from which one can draw the
conception that the sexual act is a species of communion
with the holy spirit—which is the feminine principle of the
universe).  Lawrence had apparently been led by his
discovery of the Bacchæ of Euripides in 1910 into an
exploration of the worlds which were fascinating W. B.
Yeats.  In a letter to Mrs. Nancy Henry in 1918 he writes :

> Try and get hold of Madame Blavatsky's books, they are
> big and expensive, the friends I used to borrow them from are
> out of England now.  But get from some library or other

*Isis Unveiled,* and better still the two volume work whose name I forget. Rider the publisher of *The Occult Review*—try that—publishes all these books.

These various strands from occultism are interwoven with some extremely superficial interpretations of Freudian theory. Freud's theories were not taken by him to be an " as if " basis for a therapeutic method, nor did he understand the master's account of the Œdipus complex as a generalised description of one type of neurotic pattern among many, but as a law of the relationship of fathers, mothers and sons.

> And in the woman is the eternal continuance, and from the man, in the human race, comes the exclamation of joy and astonishment at a new self-revelation, revelation of that which is woman to a man.
>
> Now every woman, according to her kind, demands that a man shall come home to her with joy and weariness of the work he has done during the day : that he shall then while he is with her be reborn of her, that in the morning he shall go forth with his new strength.
>
> But if the man does not come home to a woman, leaving her to take account of him, but is a stranger to her . . . then she shall expel him from her house as a drone. . . . For in the flesh of the woman does God exact himself. And out of the flesh of woman does he demand " Carry this me forth to utterance." And if the man deny or be too weak, then shall the woman find another man, of greater strength. And if because of the Word, which is the Law, she do not find another man, nor he another woman, then shall they both be destroyed. For he, to get that rest, and warmth and nourishment which he should have got from her, his woman, must consume his own flesh and so destroy himself : whether with wine or other kindling. And she, either her surplus shall wear away her flesh, in sickness, or in lighting up and illuminating old dead words, or she shall spend it in fighting with her man to make him take her, or she shall turn to her son and say, " Be you my Go-between."
>
> But the man who is Go-between from Woman to Production

is the lover of that woman. And if that Woman be his mother,
then is he her lover in part only ; he carries for her, but is never
received into her for his confirmation and renewal, and so
wastes himself away in the flesh. The old son-lover was
Œdipus. The name of the new one is legion. And if a
son-lover take a wife, she is only his bed. And his life will
be torn in twain, and his wife in her despair shall hope for sons,
that she may have her lover in her hour.

The ideas outlined in this passage were later developed by
Lawrence to include the idea of a collective individual, but
they were not substantially modified in any other respect.
As mysticism the foreword is easy to criticise ; it is a very
practical mystic who, when he has run away with someone
else's wife, receives a revelation of that character. What is
important about the foreword in conjunction with the letter
to Collings is that Lawrence in writing them shows that he
is torn between being a religious leader and artist ; in it he
can be seen abandoning any æsthetic or literary approach to
his writing in order to concentrate on his message.

In April 1913 Frieda and Lawrence briefly visited Rome
and Verona on their way to Irschenhausen in the familiar
Isar valley near Munich. From his brother-in-law's summer
house in the pinewoods he wrote as reassuringly as he could
to Edward Garnett, who had not taken the foreword well
and had written to say he hoped that Lawrence's new book
would not be about his relations with Frieda :

> I know I can write bigger stuff than any man in England.
> And I have to write what I can write. And I write for men
> like David and Harold—they will read me soon. My stuff is
> what they want : when they know what they want. You
> wait. . . .

He had carried *The Rainbow*, under the provisional title of
*The Sisters*, to a hundred and eighty of its planned three

hundred pages, and he had written two hundred pages of *The Lost Girl*, which then had *The Insurrection of Miss Houghton* as its provisional title.

> I can only write what I feel pretty strongly about : and that, at present, is the relation between men and women. After all, it is the problem of to-day, the establishment of a new relation, or the readjustment of the old one, between men and women.

This declaration of purpose is repeated in a letter to A. D. Macleod, an old friend on the staff of the Davidson Road Schools, who had sent Lawrence a parcel of books which included Wells' *New Machiavelli* :

> Pray to your Gods for me that *Sons and Lovers* shall succeed. People should begin to take me seriously now. And I do so break my heart over England when I read the *New Machiavelli*. And I am so sure that only through a readjustment between men and women, and a making free and healthy of this sex will she get out of her present atrophy. Oh, Lord, and if I don't "subdue my art to a metaphysic," as somebody very beautifully said of Hardy, I do write because I want folk, English folk, to alter, and have more sense.

But if he wanted to be a messiah for the English folk he didn't want to be involved with them, or to have anything to do with their lives. He couldn't bear the idea of having to come back to England to live ; and when he returned here in late June 1913 he felt himself on alien ground and was gone again by the first week in August.

## CHAPTER III

D URING his flying visit to England Lawrence met Middleton Murry and Katherine Mansfield : they had written to Lawrence that spring asking him to contribute to their poetry magazine called *Rhythm*; Lawrence was attracted by their letter, thought they sounded nice crazy people, and arranged a meeting for when he should come to England. They met when the Lawrences were spending a few days in London between their stay at the Cearne, Edward Garnett's cottage at Edenbridge, in Kent, and a boarding-house in Kingsgate, a small resort on the shoulder of the North Foreland, uneasily preserving its identity between the suburbs of Margate and Broadstairs. Lawrence took to Murry, imagining him to be a successful writer with a real creative gift, and asked him down to Kingsgate with Katherine for the following week-end. But they didn't take the invitation seriously, and in any case hadn't the money for such a jaunt, so they just didn't appear. Lawrence was furious with Murry for this weakness and wrote scolding him :

> Oh but why didn't you come and let us lend you a pound ?
> I think when times have been so rough you shouldn't bring
> about a disappointment on yourselves, just for the money.
> That seems to me wrong. We could just as well lend you
> five pounds as have it in the bank—if you want it. I consider
> now that your not coming on Sunday was a piece of obtuseness
> on your part. You are one of the people who should have a
> sense of proportionate values ; you ought to know when it is
> worth while to let yourself borrow money. Because you must
> save your soul, and Mrs. Murry's soul, from any further hurts,
> for the present, and any disappointments, or any dreary stretches
> of misery.

Lawrence with this nerved them to come for a week-end, which they enjoyed, so far as they could. But they were frightened when he tried to get them to come out to Italy for the winter : Murry apparently was so wedded to the idea of his failure to achieve anything as a writer that he couldn't consider the possibility of earning anything, and he didn't like to ask Katherine to finance the adventure out of her allowance of a hundred a year. But just as they had accepted the first week-end invitation, so they promised to come out to Italy. The adventuring spirit that could take Frieda and Lawrence over the Alps into an unknown foreign country with nothing but twenty-three pounds and their natural self-confidence was quite foreign to them ; so indeed was almost everything which made Lawrence what he was, and it is strange that he should have tried so hard to win them as disciples.

Lawrence and Frieda left England for the lodge in the pinewoods at Irschenhausen, and after a brief stay there, separated. Lawrence couldn't face the Richthofens at Baden, but having parted Frieda from her children didn't like to part her from her parents also ; he got on well with Frieda's mother and didn't in the least wish to keep them apart. But the banging on the drum of the military background he couldn't face, so while Frieda stayed in Baden he walked south, through Switzerland and the Great St. Bernard this time, into Italy. They joined forces again at the Albergo Delle Palme at Lerici, and stayed there till they found a little villa in an out-of-the-way fishing village nearby. Life was extremely hard ; the house had three bare rooms and its kitchen, money was tight and there was a long uphill climb to the post anxiously seeking cheques which didr arrive ; the divorce was still dragging on ; Frieda at times lay prostrate with agony about the children ; and there were painful scenes with members of the local Anglo-American community when Lawrence and Frieda owned to being unmarried. The happiness of the first winter by Lake Garda was, according to Frieda's memoir of twenty years later, repeated, but the occasional quarrels of that time had given place to storms of violent passionate rage which their principles forbade them to check in any way, and Frieda—one suspects—had come to rather enjoy a good paroxysm. It was during this period that the habit of spectacular rowing, which later appalled so many of their friends and acquaintances, was formed and established as part of the family ritual.

Frieda gives a picture of the end of one row which took place while Lawrence was carrying on a correspondence with Edward Marsh about the structure and technique of poetry. Lawrence, to escape her, rushed down through the olive trees in front of the house to the seashore, and pushed off in his skiff. Frieda, lagging in pursuit, arrived as he passed out of reach through the surf on to the waters of the bay of Spezia, in which Shelley's boat capsized, and yelled in her rage, " If you can't be a real poet, you'll drown like one anyhow."

Lawrence was spending a great deal of his time on the bay in this little boat, watching with an alert eye the shipping moving along the coast to Genoa, the coming and going of the fishermen, and the increasingly frequent gunnery practice of the Italian fleet. But he was not able to interpret that sullen booming over the sea as the warning it was. He saw nothing in the world big enough to really challenge him, the gunfire only made him wonder how the Italian Government could afford to blow away such quantities of powder. He pressed on, and completed a draft of *The Rainbow* ; he quarrelled with Edward Garnett about its attempt to alter his countrymen's approach to sex ; he tried to convince Edward Marsh that he was a serious poet ; and he tried to save Murry's soul :

> Get up, lad, and be a man for yourself. It's the man who dares to take, who is independent, not he who gives. I think Oxford did you harm. It's beautiful, wonderful, here. A ten pound note is 253 lire. We could get you, I believe, a jolly nice apartement in a big garden, in a house alone, for eighty lire a month. Don't waste yourself—don't be silly and floppy. You know what you could do—you could write—then prepare yourself : and first make Katherine at rest in her love for you. Say, " this I will certainly do "—it would be a relief for her to hear you. Don't be a child—don't keep that rather childish charm. Throw everything away, and say, " Now I act for my own good, at last."

And at the end of the winter of storms everything seemed to be coming Lawrence's way : Weekley's divorce proceedings were completed, *The Rainbow* was put in a fit state to be offered to a publisher, an American publisher was printing his play *The Widowing of Mrs. Holroyd*, and Garnett was arranging for the publication of a volume of short stories (it was later given the title *The Prussian Officer* in a catchpenny moment which annoyed Lawrence a good deal—he wanted it called *Goose Fair*) : they seemed to have the world at their feet, and in the first week of June set out for a holiday month in England.

Frieda went first for a fortnight with her family at Baden, while Lawrence, with an engineer from the Vickers-Maxim works at Spezia for company, walked through Switzerland and into France. When they reached London the current still seemed setting fast in their direction. Lawrence was

happy, successful and flatteringly lionised. He dropped into
Methuen's office to sign the agreement for *The Rainbow* on
his way to lunch with Lady St. Helier. Another publisher
wanted him to write a critical study of Thomas Hardy's
work, a theatrical manager was discussing a production of
*The Widowing of Mrs. Holroyd.* And on 13th July he married
Frieda at the Kensington Registrar's office—a formality
which meant a great deal to him and really made him well
content. His London host, Gordon Campbell—an Irish
lawyer—Murry, Katherine Mansfield and Catharine Carswell
formed a gay, admiring inner circle of friends round him ;
and Edward Marsh fed him on interesting people, promising
young men like Rupert Brooke and men of established
reputation. At the end of July Lawrence went off on a
walking tour in the Lakes with Koteliansky and two other
men :

> I had been walking in Westmorland rather happy, with
> water lilies twisted round my hat—big, heavy, white and gold
> water lilies that we found in a pool high up—and girls who
> were out on a spree and who were having tea in the upper
> room of an inn, shrieked with laughter. And I remember also
> we crouched under the loose wall on the moors and the rain
> flew by in streams, and the wind came rushing through the
> chinks in the wall behind one's head, and we shouted songs,
> and I imitated music hall turns, whilst the other men crouched
> under the wall and I pranked in the rain on the turf in the
> gorse, and Koteliansky groaned Hebrew music—Ranani
> Sadekim Badanoi [*sic*].
>
> It seems like another life—we were happy—four men. Then
> we came down to Barrow-in-Furness, and saw that war was
> declared.

The situation changed abruptly. The pot of gold at the
foot of *The Rainbow* melted away. Lawrence discovered
Methuens weren't bound to pay him until the book was

published—and the war might delay that indefinitely ; he found himself living more precariously than ever on his poems, short stories and sketches. He and Frieda had to leave London to economise, and they settled with Murry and Katherine Mansfield, as neighbours to Mary and Gilbert Cannan in Bellingdon Lane, Chesham, Buckinghamshire.

Lawrence began to follow more and more private lines of thought about the war. As he withheld himself from the great herd activity of the war he began to hate the herd, the mass, more and more. It was not that he was altogether a conscientious objector—though at times, as when he registered his taking of an eternal vow not to fire a shot, even if he should be shot, he obviously thought on those lines—but he was against the surrender of individual minds and bodies to anything as dead as a military machine. He was married to a German, he liked living in Italy and Italian living, he detested English ways and the timidity of English people, so that the patriotic issue meant little or nothing to him. The important things in life were problems of individual relationships, states and social organisations were necessities—like backhouses—and as long as they worked efficiently it didn't matter much what pattern you had. It wasn't in the least important if Britain was engulfed by Germany, or Germany by Britain, but it was very important that Britain and Germany shouldn't begin to engulf their individuals. The state was made for man, not man for the state—that was the important thing.

He even began to change in appearance as if to mark himself off : in 1914 only the brilliance of his wonderful eyes marked him out as an exceptional figure, he was conventional in dress and appearance, with a clean-shaven chin, a neat moustache and an ordinary haircut, neat tie and tiepin. But in 1915 he had adopted bohemian clothes, a manner of parting his reddish hair dead centre, and a beard. He had let the beard grow in the first place when he was ill in October of 1914, but it stayed always after that ; if with varying importance, sometimes it was just a beard, sometimes it was a symbol of his Messiahship. It was probably that in early 1915, because he was then recruiting disciples.

In January he moved from Chesham to a very lovely cottage at Greatham, near Pulborough, in Sussex, lent him by Viola Meynell ; and he began to spread the idea of Rananim outside the intimate circle of his close friends. He had been talking Rananim with them for months ; they were to get away from England to found an island community where they would establish a new pattern of life, that would spread, and spread, until the world was regenerated and ennobled. It was a mixture of a plan for retreat, and a plan for attack—immediately it was a plan for getting away from England and the war. It was a very complete thing in Lawrence's mind—it even had its symbol, " a phœnix, . . . rising on symmetrical wings, from a circle of very beautiful flickering flames that rose upwards from the rim of the cup." But though it was complete in Lawrence's mind, it was planned without any relation whatever to the worldly realities.

Lawrence wrote first to an old Eastwood friend, W. E. Hopkin, saying :

> We will also talk of my pet scheme. I want to gather together about twenty souls and sail away from this world of war and squalor to found a little colony where there shall be no money but a sort of communism so far as all necessaries of life go, and some real decency. It's to be a colony built up

on the real decency which is in each member of the community. A community which is established upon the assumption of goodness in the members, instead of the assumption of badness.

His next approach was to Lady Ottoline Morrell, whose husband was a Member of Parliament, and a wealthy landowner, who enjoyed a very agreeable and amusing life entertaining artists, writers and wits at Garsington Manor, her beautiful house near Oxford.

> I want you to form the nucleus of a new community which shall start a new life amongst us—a life in which the only riches is integrity of character. . . . It is communism based, not on poverty but on riches, not on humility but on pride, not on sacrifice but on complete fulfilment in the flesh of all strong desire, not in heaven but on earth. We will be the Sons of God who walk here on earth, not bent on getting and having, because we know we inherit all things. We will be aristocrats, and as wise as the serpent in dealing with the mob. For the mob shall not crush us nor cry us to death. We will deal cunningly with the mob, the greedy soul, we will gradually bring it into subjection.

And through Lady Ottoline he made an extraordinary attempt to win Bertrand Russell, wholly alien in habit of mind and ideas, into the group.

At about the same time he embarked on the conversion of Lady Cynthia Asquith, and though it was apparently never his idea that she should become one of the sacred band of twenty, he made the doctrines of Rananim specially clear for her. He began from the cloud of fire in May :

> For yourself, you must learn to believe in God. Believe me, in the end, we will unite in our knowledge of God. Believe me, this England, we very English people, will all join together and say : " We will not do these things because in our knowledge of God we know them wrong. . . . We shall agree . . . that England does not care only to have the Greatest Empire

and the greatest commerce, but that she does care supremely
for the pure truth of God, which she will try to fulfil."

But in July he was out of the cloud and down on the earth
pegging out the ground plan for the city of God :

> I hope, after the war, we may have a real revolution. I want
> the whole form of Government changing. I don't believe in
> the democratic (republican) form of election. I think the
> artisan is fit to elect for his immediate surroundings but for no
> ultimate Government. The electors for the highest places
> should be the Governors of the bigger districts—the whole
> thing should work upwards, every man voting for that which
> he more or less understands through contact—no canvassing
> of mass votes. And women shall not vote equally with men,
> but for different things. Women must govern such things as
> the feeding and housing of the race. And if a system works
> up to a Dictator who controls the greater industrial side of
> the national life, it must work up to a Dictatrix who controls
> the things relating to private life. And the women shall have
> absolutely equal voices with regard to marriage, custody of
> children, etc. There will inevitably come a revolution during
> the next ten years. I only don't want the democratic party
> to get the control. We must not have Labour in power,
> any more than Capital. I want you to agree to these things,
> vitally; because we must prepare the way for them in the
> autumn.

The stench of this particular brew of poison has become
so familiar that it is easy to overlook Lawrence's prescience
in 1915, when Mussolini was still a Socialist and Hitler
nothing very much in the German Army. But if Lawrence
intuitively foresaw the direction in which the current of
history was flowing, and dreamed of playing a big historical
rôle, he was utterly without the stamina, and the gift of
winning and keeping adherents, that were essential if the
dreams were to become action. Within a fortnight of
writing the letter to Lady Cynthia Asquith outlining the

structure of the corporate state he was to create he wrote again, already defeated and accepting defeat. Murry, Russell, everybody, even Frieda—with her optimism and her acceptance of things as they were—were traitors and Judases; he was betrayed and lost: " I had hoped to get a little nucleus of living people together. But I think it's no good. . . ."

He moved to Byron Villas in the Vale of Health, Hampstead, in August, planning to live there through the winter while he co-operated with Murry in producing a magazine called *The Signature*. He pretended later on that the paper was all Murry's idea, and that he'd no great hopes of it, but in September he was writing to all his friends saying that " It is really something: the seed I hope, of a great change in life; the beginning of a new religious era, from my point." And he obviously did pour himself—everything he believed—with complete sincerity into the essay called " The Crown " which he wrote for the magazine, perhaps so much so that he had nothing left for it—at least he lost all interest in the project thereafter and let it die. London he found as hideously depressing as he always did, and by the beginning of November all he was really interested in was escape. An acquaintance had offered him haven on an estate at Fort Myers in Florida, and he was eager to be off. In his desperation to get passports, to get money for the passage, and to get out, and clear away, he paid little attention to the publication of *The Rainbow*. He had rather lost interest in that, too—the final revision for the press had taken him much longer than usual, and there had been drawn-out argument with Pinker—his agent—and Methuens about the advisability of cutting out various, possibly objectionable, passages. Lawrence felt it was part of the past, something he was finished with—he was moving on to new things :

> To-day I have got our passports. I feel as if really we were going to America—and soon. . . . I feel awfully queer and trembling in my spirit, because I am going away from the land and the nation I have belonged to—departing, emigrating, changing the land of my soul as well as my mere domicile. It's rather terrible, a form of death. But I feel as if it were my fate—I must : to live.

## CHAPTER IV

IN the last week of October W. L. George saw that Methuen's advertisements of *The Rainbow* had abruptly disappeared ; and when he telephoned to ask why, was told that the police were acting against the book. Methuens had not bothered to tell Lawrence, and George broke the news to him. A few days later the magistrates decided the book was obscene and ordered the recall, and destruction, of all copies. The Nightmare, described in *Kangaroo*, had begun.

Although there was no money, and although the authorities made it perfectly clear that Lawrence—with or without his German wife—wouldn't be allowed out of England on any pretext, he continued to build his hopes on escape to Fort Myers and the Florida sunshine. Rananim was revived in a new form, this time not as a political venture or leadership school, but as a place where " we make songs and poems and stories and dramas, in a Vale of Avalon, in the Hesperides, among the loves." In his dream he populated it with an extraordinary company : Koteliansky, Mark Gertler, Dorothy Brett, Bertrand Russell (though he was still being difficult and intellectually stubborn), Subrawardy (an Indian who combined a bohemian good time with a certain amount of mysticism), Philip Heseltine (a musician who used the pseudonym Peter Warlock), Kouzoumdjian (a young Armenian writer whose later development as Michael Arlen showed that he had really very little in common with Lawrence), and Aldous Huxley. Throughout the decline of the year this dream kept Lawrence going ; it

45

was, in his mind, never more than a fortnight or three weeks
before they would be off, and so they gave up their flat,
sold their furniture, packed their trunks and waited.

They went to spend Christmas with Lawrence's sisters at
Ripley in Derbyshire before moving into a cottage at
St. Meryns, near Padstow, in Cornwall, lent them by J. D.
Beresford.   It shook Lawrence to find himself again in
contact with the mining community he'd left behind him
with his youth, and his thought was turned once again into
its political channel.

> Altogether the life here is so dark and violent ; it all happens
> in the senses, powerful and rather destructive : no mind, nor
> mental consciousness, unintellectual . . . These men, whom I
> love so much—and the life has such a power over me—they
> understand mentally so horribly : only industrialism, only
> wages, and money and machinery.  They can't think anything
> else.  All their collective thinking is in those terms only.  They
> are utterly unable to appreciate any pure, ulterior truth : only
> this industrial—mechanical—wage idea. . This they will act
> from—nothing else.  That is why we are bound to get some-
> thing like Guild-Socialism in the long run, which is a reduction
> to the lowest terms—nothing higher than that which now is,
> only lower.  But I suppose things have got to be reduced to
> their lowest terms—Only, Oh God, I don't want to be
> implicated in it.  It is necessary to get the germ of a new
> development towards the highest—not a reduction to the
> lowest.  That we must do, in Cornwall and Florida, the germ
> of a new era . . . we go to Cornwall, on Thursday.  There
> is the beginning.

But it wasn't really.   It was a retreat.   Cornwall was as
much of an escape as could be managed while passport
controls strangled the ports.   It was the nearest thing to
going abroad that he could contrive, but it wasn't the place
of comfort and refuge he was looking for.   The gulls
screamed at him in the wind that drove over the bare treeless

hills, and the grey breakers drove in on to the black iron rocks noisily all night and all day. It wore him down physically and mentally.

> I wish we could go a long voyage, into the South Pacific. I wish that very much. But I suppose it cannot happen. I am afraid now of America. I am afraid of the people. I daren't go there. My will won't carry me either. So I don't know what will happen. The money will last us a month or two. Something in me is asleep and doesn't trouble. . . . The only thing to be done is either to go down with the ship, sink with the ship, or, as much as one can leave the ship and like a castaway live a life apart. As for me, I do not belong to the ship ; I will not, if I can help it, sink with it.

With the spring of 1916 his spirits rose again, a project of Heseltine's—to print and publish *The Rainbow* privately—stirred him, and a change from St. Meryns to Zennor, near St. Ives, cheered him up. He began work on a new novel and wrote cheerfully to Lady Cynthia Asquith to tell her how his castaway philosophy was developing :

> One has a certain order inviolable in one's soul. There one sits as in a crow's nest out of it all. And even if one is conscripted, still I can sit in my crow's nest of a soul and grin. Life mustn't be taken seriously any more, at least, the outer social life. The social being I am has become a spectator . . . but I should be mortally indignant if I lost my life or even too much of my liberty by being dragged into the knockabout farce of this social life.

The crow's nest was tested to the utmost in the following year. Lawrence with his beard and his open defeatism (like many Frenchmen in 1939–40 he believed in defeat as a possible purge of evil in the defeated) was by himself an object of suspicion. Then various conscientious objectors among his friends came to live with him or in the neighbourhood, and the Murrys came to live in the next cottage. It was a conspicuous dissenting community—and Frieda was German. The cottage was in plain sight of the shipping lane up the Channel, and the U-boat campaign was increasing in intensity. The Lawrences were a gift to the local spy maniacs : presently they found people lying under the windows on summer nights eavesdropping ; they were ringed about with amateur spies. Towards the end of 1916 the Lawrences were reported to Scotland Yard and thereafter listed as undesirable people. The amateur spies were replaced by real detectives, and at various times the house was searched and Frieda exposed to the disagreeable humiliations which the English love to visit on foreigners. In October 1917 the Military ordered Lawrence to quit Cornwall within three days ; they didn't care where he went so long as it was out of the coastal zone. It infuriated Lawrence : he had been so proudly saying he was finished with England, and that he was a spectator watching the knockabout farce in which the body-social was so fatuously engaged. Now it became clear to him that he had been picked for the rôle of butt in the farce, and that, far from striding through the disorder like a true aristocrat, he was in there being hustled about by the clowns.

And though the wooden-faced soldiers and policemen in his house, reading his private letters, looking at his manuscripts, poking and sniffing round Frieda's foreignness, were bad enough, there were worse things. Principally the medical examination which was, for him, the real sting in conscription. Lawrence might not so very much have minded being asked to do something, or even ordered to do it. But he couldn't bear the idea of standing naked in a herd of men before the doctors to be looked at, he could bear it much less when they fingered his private parts and made him bend forward so that they could look at his arse. So far as he was concerned the dignity of his soul was wound up inextricably with the dignity of his body : this was an attempt to murder it.

The year at Zennor had been exacting in other ways. More friends had failed him. Kouzoumdjian, already turning into Michael Arlen, had vanished after a brief experimental visit ; Heseltine had developed a violent enmity to Lawrence ; and Murry had turned out not to be a friend but " an obscene bug, sucking my life away." Lawrence had even drawn away from Frieda, and often left her alone, day after day, from dawn till dusk, while he worked on a nearby farm. He imagined that everyone hated him, and found a certain comfort in hating back.

They fled out of Cornwall, leaving all their things behind them, and found refuge in Hilda Aldington's flat in Mecklenburgh Square, in London. But despair was not so complete that it ruled out dreams, and the change as usual gave Lawrence a feeling of excitement and optimism. He wrote to Cecil Gray in Cornwall to say :

> I am not anxious to come back just now. One seems to be, in some queer way, vitally active here. And then, people, one or two, seem to give a strange new response.

He began to simmer with hopes of Rananim again, in a new place, with new people. This time it was to be on the slopes of the Andes, in the Cauca Valley, by the town of Popayan, in Colombia. The sacred band was to include Lawrence, Frieda, Dr. and Mrs. Eder (owners of the land on which the colony was to be established), William Henry, Cecil Gray, Hilda Aldington, Koteliansky, Dorothy Yorke,

and perhaps Catherine and Donald Carswell. But London
and the appearance of detectives from the Special Branch of
the C.I.D., produced the inevitable reaction. After spending a
few days at the end of December with his sister Ada at Ripley
in Derbyshire, the Lawrences went down to Chapel Farm
Cottage, Hermitage, near Newbury, in Berkshire. From
there Lawrence tried to keep the new Rananim group
together for a time, and tried to add Montague Shearman
and Mark Gertler to it: but by March 1918 he realised
that none of them had anything in common with each other
let alone with him, and he abandoned the whole idea:

> I feel like a wild cat in a cage—I long to get out into some
> sort of free, lawless life—at any rate, a life where one can move
> about and take no notice of anything. I feel horribly mewed
> up. I don't want to act in concert with any body of people.
> I want to go by myself—or with Frieda—something in the
> manner of a gypsy, and be houseless and placeless and homeless
> and landless. I hate and abhor being stuck on to any form of
> society.

Savagely at odds with the world Lawrence now had to
turn to the world and beg. The police interference with
*The Rainbow* had made him suspect with publishers, the
ideas which he expressed in his articles and essays were those
which had brought him up against the Special Branch, and
his poetry was so extreme in form that he could only find
publishers among the little reviews and magazines which
couldn't pay him adequately. J. B. Pinker had done everything he could for him, but he couldn't do much beyond
an occasional five or ten pounds now and again. Lawrence
found himself beginning 1918 with just over six pounds and
no prospects. He had to go cap in hand to the Royal
Literary Fund, and although it had seen him through his

1914 crisis, help from this source now seemed an unbearable humiliation—perhaps because in the end the C.I.D. and the Royal Literary Fund are different aspects of the same thing.

In May he moved from Newbury to Mountain Cottage, at Middleton-by-Wirksworth, in the Derbyshire hills. A place as wild as Cornwall, but near his own country, and so, up to a point, healing. He was working on his *Studies in Classical American Literature*, and after reading Gibbon's *Decline and Fall* began *Movements in European History* for the Oxford University Press. With his historical studies he revived the ideas behind Rananim, but his pessimism killed the Messianic impulse that they'd nourished four years earlier.

> The chief feeling is, that men were always alike, and always will be, and one must view the species with contempt first and foremost, and find a few individuals, if possible,—which seems at this juncture not to be possible—and ultimately, if the impossible were possible, to rule the species. It is proper ruling they need, and always have needed. But it is impossible, because they can only be ruled as they are willing to be ruled ; and that is swinishly or hypocritically.

That feeling of sour disillusionment, and dislike, lasted and made Lawrence feel that he was through not merely with England, but with Europe itself. Mental exhaustion led to physical collapse, and Lawrence was ailing through the winter : sick enough to be almost indifferent to the ending of the war. All it meant was that there was at last an ultimate prospect of an end to the passport regulations. It must be remembered, though, that his master idea can be set against this apparent indifference. The war was merely a minor symptom of the ailment destroying Europe, and the end of declared war meant little—it was only a pause.

Through spring and summer and into autumn Lawrence was waiting, with bags packed, to get out. For a time at Chapel Farm Cottage again, then nearby at Ginsbury Farm, then once more at the cottage. At last, at the end of September, Frieda's passport was issued and they set out. Frieda went to her parents in Germany and Lawrence went to Lerici to wait for her.

But there were no old threads to be taken up at Lerici ; the war had changed Italy and the old spirit seemed gone. Lawrence moved to Florence and spent an odd time in a boarding-house on the Lungarno with Norman Douglas and the pathetic and sinister little person called Maurice Magnus. Perhaps because this company was so much not of Lawrence's kind he found Florence a vile place. As soon as Frieda rejoined him he moved on to Rome, and finding that no more agreeable, on again to a farm at Picinisco, near Caserta, for the end of December. Its bare savagery scared them badly, and in January 1920 they went over to Capri, to find that infected by a gossipy Anglo-American villa set, and impossible. Lawrence completed the *Movements in European History*, began the final revision of *Women in Love*, started to reanimate *The Lost Girl*, and began to pour out short stories. He was healing his mind and becoming happy again, but he was still dreaming of escape. The Andes plan was dead ; Dr. Eder had become a Zionist and was trying to woo Lawrence to Palestine, but his eyes were on more remote prospects ; the South Seas, or Africa—he thought of advertising in the *Nairobi Herald* for someone to take him as a partner on share-cropping terms.

That spring the sun really began to climb up the sky, and the soil grew kind and warm. Lawrence and Frieda escaped the close gossip circle of Capri and found a lovely house built for a Dutch couple at Fontana Vecchia, near Taormina, in Sicily. It was the first really comfortable house Frieda had been mistress of for years, and her domestic side was a good deal heartened by its blue-tiled kitchen. And she was becoming Frieda again, and not a rather frightened alien, free on sufferance. Then a few days after they settled in, prolonged negotiations with Martin Secker came to an end, and Lawrence accepted an agreement that gave him solid financial ground under his feet. Secker agreed on fair royalties and a hundred pounds' advance for Lawrence's next five novels—the amended *Rainbow* to be accepted as the first. The only fly in the ointment was Magnus, he'd decided the Lawrences were good spunging material and he pursued them with indomitable persistence and endearing bravado. While they were in Capri he'd sent Lawrence an SOS from Monte Cassino—he was in terrible trouble and without a friend to help, suicide seemed the only way . . . Lawrence went over and rescued him with a loan ; then when the Lawrences crossed over to Sicily he followed and put up at the best hotel in Taormina. He fooled Lawrence into another loan on the pretext that terrible trouble was again about to overwhelm him in Palermo, and that he must get away to Malta. He crossed on the same boat with them, and at one stage on the voyage they, travelling frugally in the second class, looked up and saw him lounging easily on the rail of the first-class deck talking to a British naval officer. He was every inch a gentleman, and a great bother to the Lawrences even after his troubles at last overwhelmed him in Malta and he really had to kill himself after all. He left his affairs in a great muddle, and gave instructions that left both Norman Douglas and Lawrence under the impression they were the literary executors ; the brisk dispute which followed led in 1924 to Douglas' remarkable pamphlet, *D. H. Lawrence and Maurice Magnus, a plea for better manners* : one of the more damaging criticisms of Lawrence.

But apart from that it was a happy year. The first three of Secker's novels were finished ; and *Aaron's Rod* begun ; most of the poems for *Birds, Beasts and Flowers* were written ; and a trip to Sardinia in the end of December and early January 1921 produced *Sea and Sardinia*. Lawrence expanded in genial directions and began work on a comic novel, *Mr. Noon*. But in March there was an ominous sign, when the Oxford University Press published Lawrence's history book under the name of Lawrence H. Davidson. And then in the summer Secker began to have doubts, and insisted on a revision of the agreement so that if *The Rainbow* were again proceeded against the costs should be borne by Lawrence. He was still cast for the butt's rôle in the knockabout farce.

The storm broke in September when *Women in Love* was published. Lawrence was at Fontana Vecchia recovering from a tiring and rather vexing summer. It had begun with Frieda being called to Baden to her mother's bedside in April. They were kept there until July while she made a slow recovery ; then they tried family life with the Schreibershofens at Thumersbach, by Zell-am-See, near Salzburg. Frieda liked living with her younger sister and her family, but Lawrence couldn't bear it. Then they went down to Florence where they had a flat looking over the stinking bed of the Arno, low with the dry summer of 1921. The Lawrences were cold-shouldered by the local equivalent of the county set, and their friends quarrelled round them. The Carswells walked over the Alps to Florence and

appeared very much Wandervögel in the urban setting :
they were fiercely jealous of the elegance of Mrs. Gilbert
Cannan—Catherine Carswell had a specially bitter pill to
swallow when she discovered that Lawrence was attentively
revising a book Mary Cannan had written about her pet
dogs. To Frieda's satisfaction Lawrence turned away from
his old friends towards the Brewsters, new, less fiercely
jealous and possessive, American acquaintances, who were
about to leave for Ceylon to study Buddhism. Then after
a brief, disappointing visit to Siena, they went back to their
home at Fontana Vecchia.

The cuttings were waiting for him there, *John Bull* and
*The Nation and Athenæum* making common cause about
*Women in Love*. Murry in his platform used rather more
intellectual language : " The things we prize are the things
he would destroy, what is triumph to him is catastrophe to
us. He is the outlaw of modern English literature ; and
he is the most interesting figure in it. But he must be
shown no mercy." *John Bull* simply translated this into
gutter language : " A book the police should ban—loathsome
study of sex depravity—misleading youth to unspeakable
disaster." At times the language used was identical : *John
Bull* called it an " obscene study," Murry said in *The Nation
and Athenæum* that Lawrence was " deliberately, incessantly,
and passionately obscene in the exact sense of the word."
And while the mud-slingers were at work in public, Heseltine
was at work privately, playing on Secker's fears of police
action and inducing him to have a number of passages
hacked out of the book. He pretended he'd been libelled
in the name of Halliday in it, and he worked like a beaver
till he got his cuts—and fifty pounds—out of Secker.

Well, that was what England, and friends, meant.

Lawrence looked East : there were the Brewsters in Ceylon with their Buddhism, and there was Mabel Dodge Luhan in New Mexico offering him a place in a community of unspoiled Indians worshipping the sun in real purity of spirit. In February 1922 he slipped away, out of Europe.

## CHAPTER V

IN the excitement of departure and change Lawrence found a complete release, as usual. He fell back into love with almost everything. The ship and the service delighted him—they looked after Frieda so beautifully when she came aboard sick at Naples—and his heart even warmed towards his fellow-passengers :

> The people on board are mostly simple Australians. I believe Australia is a good country, full of life and energy. . . . If we don't want to go on living in Ceylon I shall go to Australia if we can manage it.

He sat basking, drawing content out of the sea, and amusing himself by translating an Italian dialect novel—Giovanni Verga's *Mastro don Gesualdo*.

> It is my opinion that once beyond the Red Sea one does not feel any more that tension and pressure one suffers from in England—in Europe altogether—even in America, I believe— perhaps worse there. I feel so glad I've come out. . . .

But, as usual, it didn't last : Ceylon was a washout ; and in a very short time Buddhism was done with. In the steaming heat, among elephants and palmy jungles, Lawrence began to dream of the innocent white blossom of apple trees, and the orchards of Australia.

> I feel absolutely dead off Buddhism, either Nibbana, or Nirvana, Kama or Karma. They can have Buddha. . . .

and he became rather appalled by the tensionless dark masses round him in the east ; soft-boned, voluptuous, soulless. It was all too alien.

But I do think, still more now I'm out here, that we make a mistake forsaking England and moving out into the periphery of life. After all, Taormina, Ceylon, Africa, America—as far as we go, they are only the negation of what we ourselves stand for and are : and we're rather like Jonahs running away from the place we belong. That is the conclusion that is forced on me. So I am making up my mind to return to England during the course of the summer. I really think that the most living clue of life is in us Englishmen in England, and the great mistake we make is in not uniting together in the strength of this real living clue—religious in the most vital sense—uniting together in England and so carrying the vital spark through. Because so far as we are concerned it is in danger of being quenched. I know now it is a shirking of the issue to look to Buddha or the Hindu or to our own working men, for the impulse to carry through. It's in ourselves, or nowhere, and this looking to the outer masses is only a betrayal. I think too the Roman Catholic Church, as an institution, granted of course some new adjustments to life, might once more be invaluable for saving Europe, but not as a mere political power. But this I know : the responsibility for England, the living England rests on men like you [Robert Pratt Barlow] and me and Cunard—probably even the Prince of Wales—and to leave it all to Bottomleys, etc., is a worse sin than any sin of commission.

Yet he went on, away towards Taos, by way of Australia ; the summer came and went, and he settled for the winter in Mexico. He knew his responsibility, and he knew where he belonged, but he just couldn't face it. Australia he half loved and half hated—

the country has an extraordinary hoary, weird attraction . . . it seems so old, as if it had missed all this Semite-Egyptian-Indo-European vast era of history, and was coal age, the age of great ferns and mosses. It hasn't got a consciousness—just none— too far back. . . . Often I hate it like poison, then again it fascinates me, and the spell of its indifference gets me. I can't quite explain it : as if one resolved back almost to the plant

kingdom, before souls, spirits and minds were grown at all :
only quite alive. . . .

But if Australia's untouchedness seemed to offer a tempting
way of escape to Lawrence as an individual, he was anything but tempted by a society based entirely on western
materialism, and quite untouched by the intellectual tradi-
tions of Europe.

> Talk about crude, raw, and self-satisfied. If every American
> is a King or Queen, I'm sure every Australian is a little Pope
> all on his own, God's Vicar. There's nothing better than me
> on earth he seems silently to proclaim, not with tongues of
> angels or tones of silver, either : and not always silently. I've
> got a bitter and burning nostalgia for Europe, for Sicily, for old
> civilisation and for real human understanding—not for this
> popery of sacred " convenience "—everything is so convenient
> they keep telling you. They can keep their convenience.

What Lawrence wanted to keep was in England, but still
he didn't go there. There was still one more chance at
Taos, so he left his bungalow called Wyewurk, at Thirroul,
in New South Wales, and set out for the Indian pueblo, to
find the men integrated in their worship of the sun. And
of course when he got there he found the wretched colony
of bohemians and rootless marginal-livers that he found
everywhere—existing this time not as spectators of Italian or
Austrian or English working-class life, but spectators to
Indian life. And the Indians crept out of their mud huts
to sell serapes, and pots, and magic dances to the Americans
for money. They were really Americans dressed up, under
alien masks of flesh, but the same money-poisoned Americans
underneath. The only thing that Mexico had was the desert,
the mountain desert, with the bright sun close by in the
unpolluted air : Lawrence dreamed of riding off into the

unpossessed desert, right out of the human community, into nothingness.

The Lawrences stood Taos for about eight weeks and then moved to the Del Monte Lands, seventeen miles out into the desert country. And that way of escape failed too ; all that winter he lived on the ranch, with two very nice, but very unintellectual, Danish painters as companions. It was unbelievably beautiful, and there were all the delightful country things to do—livestock to tend, horses to ride, trees to cut up for the blazing wood fires, and hot springs of the Rio Grande not far off to bathe in. It was, so far as the material side went, an extremely happy time, but there was nothing on the inside. Lawrence knew it had to come to going back to England, but instead planned to go to Russia. And he wrote *Kangaroo*—the story of an Australian Messiah who couldn't save anything or anybody.

Frieda knew he ought to come to England too and began to try to drive him. It was a fight—at first Lawrence won. He began *The Plumed Serpent*, which took them down into old Mexico, to the shores of Lake Chapala, and he said he had to stay there—it was necessary for the book. But she wore him down, and in July got him started towards home. The nearer he got to home, the less he liked the idea. In New Orleans he was already deciding he wanted to go back to Mexico, and when it came to New York he just dug in his toes and wouldn't get on the ship. Frieda went to England alone ; Lawrence bolted to Los Angeles—as far as he could get in the opposite direction on land—and presently found himself back in old Mexico at Guadalajara. He was fighting a great battle inside himself. *The Plumed Serpent* was taking shape as a statement of his mysticism ; he still stood by the rejected foreword to *Sons and Lovers* and

by the creed he had outlined in " The Crown "—the essay
written for *The Signature* ; he had restated those ideas in
the *Fantasia of the Unconscious* in 1921 and he still believed
them as strongly as ever. But in the beauty of Mexico,
and in the simple surface companionship of his Danish friend
Gotzche—who was so nice, and straightforward, and comfortable, with his interest in surfaces and appearances—he
found a terrible temptation to abandon ideas altogether. To
just be contented, and be part of the landscape, to take the
easy line, and give up, forget the mission, and the idea of
making people live in a new way. At Los Angeles he even
thought of signing on as a ship's cook in a sailing boat
bound for the Pacific Islands, if the Danes would sign on as
foremast hands. That was a new version of his recurrent
phantasy to escape to sea in his own boat. Part of his
happiness at Lerici had been having a boat, and he treasured
the memory of a run down the Lancashire coast in a fisher-
man's boat in August 1914 as one of his last enjoyments in
the free world. After the war, in Italy, he dreamed of
buying a *tartane* (just like The Rover in the Conrad novel
he despised so much), and he was always reading books like
Lord Dufferin's *Letters from High Latitudes* and feeding his
adventurous longings. It is easy for the town dweller to get
the wrong idea about Daniel Boone, the man in the coonskin
hat, the pioneer, the adventurer who goes into the wilderness
alone ; you may be admiring him for his courage most
when he's surrendering to a blue funk and flying from the
menaces and complications which make your normal life.
But here was Lawrence at Guadalajara, like the ass between
two bundles of hay, between the wilderness and normal
life.

His own work went badly. *The Plumed Serpent* coiled

and coiled round him, getting more and more obscure.
Because he was so troubled in himself he found it much
easier to get on with someone else's work, and he rewrote
a novel written by an Australian friend, *The Boy in the Bush*.
He hoped, he terribly hoped, for the live young gods to
come walking out of Lake Chapala, and he wrote doggedly
on about it. But they didn't come, and all round him the
Spanish civilisation festered and died on top of the carcass
of the Indian civilisation it had long ago murdered. Frieda
bombarded him with letters : you're English, I'm where
you belong, you'd better come too. And Middleton
Murry put his oar in : he'd started *The Adelphi*, things were
happening in England, and England needed Lawrence.
Absence makes the heart grow fonder, and so on ; Lawrence
had forgotten the " obscene bug " episode and the failure
of life with the Murrys in Cornwall, now he found himself
corresponding in a quite friendly way with Murry. Katherine
Mansfield had died and Murry was standing by himself, and
might—Lawrence thought—be able now to be a fighter and
a bit less of a love-and-sympathy hunter. Perhaps it would
be worth going to England, just to see, anyway.

Perhaps, and Lawrence tried hard to be hopeful, although
he knew just as well as when he set out that he was finished
with Europe. While he was arranging to come to England
he was drawing up his last plans for Rananim, this time in
the Mexican mountain deserts. The new people in the
plan were the Danes, Knud Merrild and Gotzche ; Witter
Bynner, a poet he had encountered in Taos ; Willard Johnson,
American literary critic who was just starting a paper called
*The Laughing Horse* ; and then there were the old friends,
Murry, Koteliansky, Gertler, the Carswells, Mary Cannan
and Dorothy Brett. This time it was going to really come

into being, the cell that would regenerate the world, there
on the Del Monte Ranch, seventeen miles outside Taos.

Lawrence sailed from Vera Cruz at the end of November
1923, and arrived in London in the first week of December.

> Here I am—London—gloom—yellow air—bad cold—bed—
> old house—Morris wall-paper—visitors—English voices—tea
> in old cups—poor D. H. L. perfectly miserable, as if he was in
> his tomb. You don't need his advice, so take it : Never come
> to Europe any more. . . .

At least his advice was perfectly sound about the Europe
he came to ; which he gathered up into a private room at
the Café Royal—the people who were to found Rananim.
They sat there, the nucleus of the new order of things, and
drank a good deal of claret.   First there was a row,
Koteliansky couldn't bear it when Lawrence and Donald
Carswell began talking bad Spanish to each other.   When
that was over Koteliansky began breaking glasses and making
a speech about Lawrence's unique greatness, and how Frieda
was the only woman capable of understanding or appreciating
it.   Then Lawrence, looking pale and ill, told them about
Rananim again, and told them that the time had come to
make it.   Who would come ?   Mary Cannan was honest
enough to say no, fair and square.   All the rest said yes,
and didn't mean it, except Dorothy Brett, who was ready
to go.   In despair Lawrence put his arm round Murry's
shoulders and said, " Do not betray me ! "   Only to get
" I love you, Lorenzo, but I won't promise not to betray
you," for his answer.   Within a few minutes Lawrence fell
forward on to the table, vomited, and passed out cold.
Mark Gertler and Mary Cannan were, suddenly, not of the
party, and the others took Lawrence back to Hampstead
like a corpse.   Frieda had been sitting watching the whole

thing going wrong from the beginning, detached, and sickened. This was the end of bringing Lawrence home, and there was no doubt about it, it was a terrible mistake. He had been right round the world, he was back at his starting-point, and it was this. Never again, never again.

This should have been a climax, it should have marked a complete break in Lawrence's life. But he had a determined stubborn streak in him, and as he'd said he was going to really make Rananim this time nothing was going to stop him. He'd given his word, and if he had only got one follower, that didn't make any difference. So after visiting Baden, and Paris, he set out. With one disciple, poor Dorothy Brett, as deaf as a post, with an ear trumpet cocked and ready in case she should miss any word from the Messiah. It was a long way back, over the Atlantic, through the wen of New York, down through the United States, and up, up, up to the Del Monte Ranch poised at eight thousand six hundred feet above the sea. And there was nothing whatever there when they got there, except the thin air, and their unregenerate hearts drumming in their rib cages. They worked like niggers, making mud bricks, rebuilding the ranch buildings, a house for Frieda and Lawrence, a shack for Brett, and making it all snug for the winter. But it wasn't Rananim at all. It was a wonderful summer living in glorious country ; just that. It was great fun riding the horses Azul and Aaron, and milking the cow Susan, and picking raspberries bravely in the drifts of canes where the bears came out of the canyon. All the happiness in the world couldn't disguise the fact that, so far from having Rananim, what they had got was the basis of the popular novel, or farce for matter of that. A common or garden triangle.

The weather broke early in the autumn and the valley began to pile up with snow, which made a good excuse for getting out and moving on.

> If the roads are passable, we shall go down to Taos on Saturday, stay a day or two, then go down to Mexico City. My spirit always wants to go south. . . . Brett will go down with us. But if we take a house, she must take a little place of her own. Not to be too close. . . .

They took a house at Oaxaca, where Lawrence wrote *Mornings in Mexico* and finished *The Plumed Serpent*, while the triangle tightened. The attempt to kick it apart by moving south had failed and the tension grew worse ; Brett was still too close—for Frieda and for Lawrence really. He kept going by blowing off steam in Murry's direction :

> I sent you a letter two days ago, and yesterday came the little yellow cry from your liver. . . . *The Adelphi* was bound to dwindle : though why not fatten it up a bit. Why in the name of hell didn't you rouse up a bit last January, and put a bit of gunpowder in your stuff, and fire a shot or two. But you preferred to be soft, and to go on stirring your own finger in your own vitals. . . . Spunk is what one wants, not introspective sentiment. The last is your vice. You rot your own manhood at the roots with it. . . .

The women, however, were not able to exploit such outlets, and in the end Frieda told Lawrence to give Brett her marching orders. It was something of a relief to Lawrence to be forced to tell her to go because his false relationship with his only disciple had been becoming increasingly irksome to him.

> No, Brett. I do not want your friendship, till you have a full relation somewhere, a kindly relation of both halves, not in part, as all your friendships have been. That which is in part is in itself a betrayal. Your " friendship " for me betrays

D.H.L.—5

the essential man and male that I am, and makes me ill. Yes, you make me ill, by dragging at one half at the expense of the other half. And I am so much better now you have gone. . . .

So Rananim, even as a mere triangle, smashed, and the dream of the sacred band that would regenerate the world perished drearily. Lawrence's heart broke. For two years, or more, he had been fighting the disease which was in him with his will ; now that his sense of purpose was destroyed his will collapsed and the disease took him. They pretended to themselves for a time that it was some local fever, they could shake it off when he was well enough to travel. But there came in the end the day when the pretence collapsed : an indifferent doctor stood by Lawrence lying in his bed and looked over to Frieda—" Mr. Lawrence has tuberculosis," he said.

## CHAPTER VI

FROM then on Lawrence was dying : it's true that any man is dying all the time, of course, and logically it should make no difference that the process has been given a name—tuberculosis, or cancer, or whatever it may happen to be.  But all the same the built-in opium pipe, the self-drugging apparatus, usually works pretty well, and it is something of a shock to a man to be given—within a month or two—the date when the clods will patter down on the coffin lid and the liquid flesh start to ooze off the bones.  It breaks something in him as a rule when he's told that the slight loss of appetite, plus the slight loss of weight, plus the slight increase in fatigue, plus the slight increase in wakefulness at night, plus the slight, faint, but constant sense of trouble in the body, add up to a total that means that he is finished.  Death crept up on Lawrence while he was in despair because his leadership venture had failed, because his one adherent had been a mere sentimental conquest—not a fellow-thinker and adventurer, and because the Indian way of life—on which he'd built such hopes—was done for and the Indians, wounded to death by the Spanish, were being finished off by the Americans.  What he had at first taken for a local disease in Taos, in New Mexico, on United States soil, was general, and worse, if anything, further south in Mexico proper.  He was depressed by Mexico City, a town which impressed him as a mean criminal meditating its next petty crime ; and depressed beyond measure by the Indians in off-the-peg suits whom he found running the municipal political rackets and dodges of democratic politics.  They

were like the worst English, the worst Europeans, an
extremely horrible to him. Overwhelmed by all th
Lawrence slid towards death, but as soon as the doctors sai
Tuberculosis, he had something to grapple with that was nc
part of his personal disaster.

In the heat and malarial stench of Oaxaca and Mexico Cit
he recovered enough to make it safe for him to travel bac
to the Del Monte Ranch in April 1925. There they foun
the place dead, shuttered, and boarded up ; but ill a
Lawrence was his home-making gift came into play, and i
a few days the cold ash of Rananim turned itself into
warm fire to re-create the phœnix. He became strong enoug
for all the old country work that he loved—tending th
stock, wood-cutting and gardening. By September he wa
as well as ever, a delicate man who had to watch his healt
certainly, but not a dying man. With his new confidenc
and health, however, his curse came on him and he felt tha
he had to go. He was perhaps a little afraid of the winte
at the great height of the ranch, and he now felt a rea
craving for the Mediterranean and Europe again ; at th
least he had to pull up his stakes and travel—he just had t
be somewhere else if he felt any danger of becoming fixed.

> I think if I had to choose, myself, between being a Duke c
> Portland or having a million sterling and forced to live up t
> it, I'd rather far, far rather, be a penniless tramp. There is dee
> inside one a revolt against the fixed thing, fixed society, fixe
> money, fixed homes, even fixed love. I believe that was wha
> ailed your brother, he couldn't bear the social fixture of every
> thing. It's what ails me too.

They left towards the end of September 1925 and wer
in England in October, motoring through his own countr
in Derbyshire between two flying visits to Bloomsbury

While Lawrence was in England he arranged a meeting with Murry which ended in a confusion typical of their relationship—with Lawrence looking for Murry in one street, and Murry looking for Lawrence in another. Lawrence wrote a somewhat teasing letter of apology when he was safely out of England in Baden :

> I'm sorry I missed you—I hurried straight to the house, on the obvious way. I had such a nice bag of fruit for you to take home with fresh figs, and dates and carlsbad plums. But perhaps you'ld have hated carrying it, so heavy. . . .

But he took the sting out of it by saying he might write a little article for *The Adelphi*, and Murry continued his attempts to woo him as a contributor. However, in the Villa Bernardo, at Spotorno, near Genoa, where Lawrence settled for the winter he sickened of Murry's writing about Jesus.

> My dear Jack, it's no good ! All you can do now, sanely, is to leave off. . . . In short, shut up. Throw *The Adelphi* to the devil, throw your own say after it . . . you've perhaps got J. M. M. on the brain even more seriously than J. C. Don't you remember, we used to talk about having a little ship ? The Mediterranean is glittering blue to-day. Bah, that one should be a mountain of mere words. Heave ho ! my boy ! Get out of it !

A few days after he received this letter Murry got his presentation copy of *Reflections on the Death of a Porcupine*, in which Lawrence rather unhandsomely disowned his enthusiasm for the magazine they started together during the war ; more than unhandsomely he went further and made a guy of Murry for undertaking such a futile gesture. It was a grand opportunity for Murry to pay Lawrence back in his own coin and he rose to it to a certain extent, getting home with one thrust which rankled—when he called Lawrence a professional heel-kicker. But inner compulsions compelled him to add to this display of manly fury an appeal to allow *The Adelphi* to print various Lawrence articles and essays for nothing—" as the gift of one man to another." It left him wide open to Lawrence's answer :

> Dear Jack—I would rather you didn't publish my things in *The Adelphi*. As man to man, if ever we were man to man, you and I, I would give them to you willingly. But as writer to writer, I feel it is a sort of self-betrayal. Surely you realise the complete incompatibility of my say with your say. Say your say, Caro !—and let me say mine. But for heaven's sake don't let us pretend to mix them.

And that was that, until right at the end of Lawrence's life Murry managed to draw on himself another north-west gale of a letter, as complete a disavowal as a man could write :

> And the me that you say you love is not me, but an idol of your own imagination. Believe me, you don't love me. The animal that I am you instinctively dislike—just as all the Lynds and Squires and Eliots and Goulds instinctively dislike it—and you all say there's no such animal, or if there is there ought not to be—so why not stick to your position ? If I am the only man in your life, it is not because I am I, but merely because I provided the speck of dust on which you formed your crystal of an imaginary man. We don't know one another—if you knew how little we know one another ! And let's not pretend. By pretending a bit we had some jolly times in the past. But we all had to pretend a bit—and we could none of us keep it up. Believe me, we belong to different worlds, different ways of consciousness, you and I, and the best we can do is to let one another alone, for ever and ever. We are a dissonance. My health is a great nuisance, but by no means as bad as all that, and I have no idea of passing out. We want to leave next week for a short tour in Spain—then go north. So don't think of coming to Mallorca. It's no good our meeting—even when we're immortal spirits, we shall dwell in different Hades. Why not accept it . . . ?

But still we had to have *Reminiscences of D. H. Lawrence*, *Son of Woman*, and the squalid argy-bargy with Catherine Carswell : it would have been better to accept it, and spare the world the spectacle of the biographer of Keats and the biographer of Burns pelting each other with mud scooped off Lawrence's grave mound.

Lawrence was in a somewhat combative mood in spring 1926 : he was exasperated because Frieda's grown-up children came out to stay with them and robbed him of some of her interest and love. He countered by laying his past on her doorstep, and asking his sister Ada and a friend to stay. It was a fierce household ; Ada was a fine English arguer of the hands-on-hips and tell-you-straight sort, and Barby Weekley was of the same tartar breed as her mother when it came to standing pat—in a very short time the whole thing blew up like a tub of gunpowder, Ada being blown back to England, and Lawrence into Capri after a few weeks of sick and solitary wandering on the mainland. Frieda remained fiercely and proudly at Spotorno, refusing to take him back until her daughters persuaded her that it was the right thing to do.

When they came together again they were extremely happy : they moved from the Gulf of Genoa down to Florence where they found, in the Villa Mirenda, at Scandicci, half an hour from the city by tram, a place where Frieda was content and where Lawrence could work. He had been upset by the cool reception England gave to *The Plumed Serpent*, but he now warmed again to work. His play *David* was being published, and he plunged into *Lady Chatterley's Lover* ; a book about the Etruscans also began to take shape. However, the soles of his feet began to itch as soon as he settled down, and in July they shot off to

Baden, to Inverness, to Mablethorpe in Lincolnshire, Sutton-on-Sea and London, returning to the Villa Mirenda in October. And all the old dreams began to stir too, of flight back to America, or to Russia, or of going back to the fight and the Messianic campaign to save England for the light. *Lady Chatterley's Lover* had its origin in the declaration of purpose he made in his letter to A. D. Macleod in 1913 : he was writing to change the English attitude to sex ; and he had still ideas of working through example. Rananim was dead, and with it the idea of the ideal community as a place of refuge—an idea implicit in its location anywhere outside England ; Lawrence was now dreaming of an ideal community in England. He developed his ideas on this subject in the course of a long correspondence with Rolf Gardiner in which he defines many of the terms he uses in a sufficiently arcane fashion elsewhere. Gardiner was then studying, with what Lawrence took to be ambitious intentions, the various German movements which had moving the mass as their aim. Lawrence told Gardiner that any intellectual approach to the mass was impossible, it could only succeed if it was an appeal to their interest of a material character, in which case the movement could only end in a frustrate situation equivalent to the existing situation. The appeal, to produce a good result, must go through the materialist surface to the fundamental good in man. The way in, he considered, was through instinctive responses, to songs, dances, and work in common ; by singing together, dancing together, and working together men could start a flow of disinterested fellowship between themselves that would be genuinely creative. Any banding together for purposes of self-interest would be poisoned from the outset by the meanness of its intention. The shadow cast by the

General Strike chilled Lawrence, he loved the miners he was brought up among as people, he couldn't bear them as strikers, or Trades Unionists, paralysing the life of the whole country for mean thoughts about money.

> If I were talking to the young, I should say only one thing to them : don't you live just to make money, either for yourself or anybody else. Try to find out what life itself is, and live. Repudiate the money idea. And then I'd teach them if I could to dance and sing together. The togetherness is important. . . . It's very difficult to do anything with the English, they have so little " togetherness " or power of " togetherness " : like grains of sand that will only fuse if lightning hits it. . . . The Germans take their shirts off and work in the hay : they are still physical ; the English are so woefully disembodied, God knows what's to do with them. I sometimes think they are too sophisticatedly civilised to have any future at all . . . the German *Bunde* I am afraid will drift into nationalistic, and ultimately fighting bodies : a new, and necessary form of militarism. It may be the right way for them. But not for the English. The English are over tender. They must have kindled again their religious sense of at-one-ness. And for that you must have a silent, central flame, a flame of consciousness and of warmth which radiates out bit by bit. Keep the core sound, and the rest will look after itself. What we need is reconciliation and atoning. I utterly agree with your song, dance, and labour ; but the core of atoning in the few must be there, if your song, dance, and labour are to be a real source. If it is possible. The German youth is almost ready to fuse into a new sort of fighting unity, it seems to me, us against the world. But the English are older, and weary even of victory.

It is easy to be seduced by the lack of true-blue patriotism in this passage and others like it into assuming that Lawrence was a Fascist. He was, no doubt, in 1915–16 when he planned out a corporate state with a social pyramid crowned by a dictator, but he had developed his ideas far beyond that.

His own failure to attract followers may have been influential in bringing about the change, but whatever their origins his feelings or his final conclusions were sound.

> I'm afraid the whole business of leaders and followers is somehow wrong, now. . . . I'm afraid part of what ails you is that you are struggling to enforce an obsolete form of leadership. When leadership has died . . . it will be born again, perhaps, new and changed, and based on a reciprocity of tenderness. The reciprocity of power is obsolete. When you get down to the basis of life, to the depth of the warm creative stir, there is no power. It is never. There shall be light !— only : Let there be light. . . .

He modified his ideas even after the completion of *The Plumed Serpent*, the reforming organisation in that book, he came to think, was too earth-bound and dirty-handed with temporal power.

> . . . about *The Plumed Serpent* and " The Hero." On the whole I think you're right. The hero is obsolete, and the leader of men is a back number. After all at the back of the hero is the militant ideal : and the militant ideal, or the ideal militant, seems to me also a cold egg. We're sort of sick of all forms of militarism and militantism, and " Miles " is a name no more, for a man. . . . And the new relationship will be some sort of tenderness, sensitive between men and men and men and women, and not the one up one down, lead on I follow, Ich Dien sort of business. . . .

But for all the astuteness, and even political wisdom, there was in one quarter of his brain there was the other quarter which was entirely blind to the outside world. Lawrence's thoroughly healthy sexual responses convinced him that during the sexual act there was a period when the gap between man's instinctive pattern of responses and his rational mind closed, when he was all of one piece—at one with his environment, at one with himself, and unegotistically united with his woman. The last point was the most important ; the conscious, daytime, or intellectual part of a man's mind was virtually incapable of a disinterested approach to a woman : it would automatically consider the future in egotistic terms. Will it be fun for me ? By thunder I'll look a dog walking down Market Street with yon bobby-dazzler ! If she can cook and look after a house, she'd be the wife for me ! And so on—this materialistic, egotistic approach could only be shed by most people in the emotional and physiological storm which rages round the sexual act, it was the only moment when a real relationship between man and woman was established. Lawrence felt that by developing the awareness of ordinary people to that momentarily disinterested relationship he could expand its duration into their conscious lives, to replace, with infinite benefit, the basis of their normal daily contact. (His parents had been so dismal together when they had nothing but the home and its concerns between them, they only existed for each other physically—suppose their successful physical relationship had been recognised as the vitally important part of their marriage, instead of a shameful annex to it, how much happier the whole thing might have been ?) Lawrence proceeded to campaign for this awareness with his blind spot resolutely covering the pink and black lace pantie side of our civilisation; the fuss about *The Rainbow* should have warned him of its befouling powers, but he went on to try to regain the naive or innocent soul by awakening the phallic consciousness.

He was not strong enough to do it. In July 1927, one hot afternoon Lawrence came into the Villa Mirenda with a great basket of peaches, plucked from the trees in the garden : they were perfect and he showed them to Frieda with delight. He set them down, and went into another room; a few minutes later Frieda ran to him at his call and found him lying down with blood running terribly from his mouth.

They went to Villach, in Austria, to get well, and after that Lawrence's life had a pattern—winter in the sun in the hot Mediterranean littoral countries, summer among the mountains to escape the heat. All the time, now, the disease was gaining, and Lawrence was pretending that he was finding the places unsuitable.

After the summer at Villach they went back to the Villa Mirenda, where Lawrence took it easily, giving most of his time to painting and to seeing *Lady Chatterley's Lover* through George Orioli's Lungarno Press. Aldous and Maria Huxley were much with him at this time, almost the only people who gave him the friendship and support he needed. His London friends were staggered by the manuscript of Lady Chatterley and her adventures: his agent, his publisher, and everyone else who saw the book begged him not to publish it. He went doggedly ahead, and out of stubbornness began to paint pictures that were more and more oblivious of the normal tabus. When the book was at last through the press, and an exhibition of his pictures arranged at the Warren Gallery in Maddox Street, London, the summer of 1928 was beginning, and they moved up into the cool dry air of the mountains at Kesselmatte, in Switzerland, to rest and get strong again.

There the trouble began. The American anti-vice societies had been exacerbated by *The Escaped Cock*, the first version of *The Man Who Died*, which combines Lawrence's views on Christ with his views on sex: they were watching in a state of yeasty excitement for what Lawrence would do next. When *Lady Chatterley's Lover* began to come to America in George Orioli's edition the various anti-vice societies brought pressure to bear on the United States Customs Authorities to induce them to seize any copies that should be sent into the country. They also made public protests against the sale of the book and attracted the attention of the pornographic book trade ; in no time photostatic reproductions of the Orioli edition began to circulate in considerable numbers. The success of these editions led to piracy of an even more undesirable kind ; publishers—if one can call them that—who were only capable of understanding the shorter words in the book began to make their own printings. In these some of the duller passages were omitted in favour of more consistently entertaining material contrived by native American writers. While all this was going on in America the massive mind of Lord Brentford, then Sir William Joynson-Hicks, was grieving in Great Britain. Sir William had given much thought, as an Imperial Englishman, to the reasons for the decline of the Roman Empire and had at the last decided that it was due to the stream of indecent literature which flowed like an open sewer through the capital. At the time British ships on the American run were regularly importing, and by the ton weight, tens of thousands of copies of magazines with such titles as *Film Frolics*, *Spicy Detective*, *Silk Stocking*, and so on, so that a problem could, fairly, be said to exist. Sir William met it by initiating a campaign against serious novels written with the intention of destroying the states of mind which lead to a craving for such literature. Scotland Yard went into action, and toured London warning booksellers not to handle *Lady Chatterley's Lover* as soon as it appeared ; preparations were made for getting a judgement

that would entitle them to seize and burn all the copies
they could reach. All that was exasperating enough for
Lawrence, but Scotland Yard were not content to leave the
matter there. Presumably the dossier compiled when
Lawrence was suspect and ordered out of Cornwall during
the war was the basis for their action, but whatever the
ostensible reasons, when Lawrence moved south for the
winter, after a short visit to Baden, the French police were
notified that an undesirable character was on his way.
When he reached La Vigie, the dismantled fortress on the
isle of Port Cros which Richard Aldington had made his
home, the place was under police observation. The old
spying days of Zennor, which had so upset him in the days
when he was ten years younger and stronger, were back.
The French police were specially useful in warning the
British authorities when bulky packets of a promising
nature were posted off Londonwards, and presently Scotland
Yard were able to gather new laurels for the British Crown
by filching the manuscripts of *Pansies* and Lawrence's essay
on painting, *An Introduction to these Pictures*, from the post.
It was exasperating, the more so because the English news-
papers which reached them on the islet were carrying
without hesitation stories which the gutter press of the
'nineties would have handled with caution ; they served up
at breakfast the latest woman bitten to death on Clapham
common, the latest dismembered torso fished out of some
slimy conduit, the latest assault, perversion, and marital
disaster. And Sir William Joynson-Hicks fought like a tiger
to protect all this sweetness and light from the corruption
of literature. Lawrence wrote to Aldous Huxley damning
him for trying to draw him as Rampion in *Point Counter
Point*, but praising the book for its general intention.

I do think that art has to reveal the palpitating moment or the state of man as it is. And I think you do that terribly. But what a moment ! And what a state ! If you can only palpitate to murder, suicide, and rape in their various degrees—and you state plainly that it is so—caro, however are we going to live through the days ? Preparing still another murder, suicide, and rape ? But it becomes a phantasmal boredom, and produces ultimately inertia, inertia, inertia, and final atrophy of the feelings. Till, I suppose, comes a final super war, and murder, suicide, rape sweeps away the vast bulk of mankind. It is as you say—intellectual appreciation does not amount to so much, it's what you thrill to. And if murder, suicide, and rape is what you thrill to, and nothing else, then it's your destiny—you can't change it mentally. You live by what you thrill to, and there's the end of it. . . .

Life became too difficult on Port Cros ; La Vigie was on the summit of the island so that any walk ended in an exhausting climb ; the storms sweeping across the Gulf of Lyons broke their full strength on it, and there was no baker so that even bread had to be brought across the tricky Hyères roadstead in an open boat. Lawrence had another flux of blood from the lungs and it became important to be within easy reach of a doctor. They moved across to Bandol on the mainland and settled into the Hotel Beau Rivage ; Lawrence lying in bed much of the time, iller than he would own, itching to get on the move again. He wanted to be off to Taos in America, to Capri, to Lake Garda, to Taormina in Sicily, to Zululand to paint Zulus.

At the end of March 1929 he went to Paris to settle some of his fascinatingly complicated business transactions with publishers, and then moved to Palma de Mallorca :

It's queer, there is a certain loveliness about the island, yet a certain underneath ugliness, unalive. The people seem to me rather dead, and they are ugly, and they have those non-existent

bodies that English people often have, which I thought wa
impossible on the Mediterranean. But they say there is a larg
Jewish admixture. Dead-bodied people with rather ugly face
and a certain staleness. . . . The Spaniards, I believe, hav
refused life so long that life now refuses them, and they ar
rancid. . . .

In June Lawrence went to Florence and Frieda went to
London to see her children and to attend the opening o
the exhibition of his paintings at the Warren Gallery. I
had been delayed so that it could be synchronised with the
publication of two editions, one at ten guineas and one a
fifty guineas, of reproductions—and publication itself hac
been delayed by the printer's reluctance to handle some o
the plates. That should have warned Lawrence, it certainl
warned Scotland Yard. At any rate they raided the gallery
seized the pictures and what books remained unsold, ther
brought them before one of the more delicate-mindec
magistrates and had them legally certificated as obscene
They also seized some drawings by a dirty-minded fellow
called William Blake in the Warren Gallery at the same
time. . . .

Lawrence went into Bavaria to escape the full heat of the
summer ; he felt sick, and spattered with filth from al
sides. Scotland Yard were fighting hard for the right to buri
the pictures they'd stolen from the Warren Gallery at one
end of the noble scale of human activity, and at the other ai
enterprising Philadelphia publisher was pirating *Lady Chatterle*
and producing it with illustrations. Unfortunately when he
was at the depth of this depression a Bavarian dietetic quack
got hold of him, and bore him off to a pseudo-sanatoriun
where they dosed him with a course of drugs—arsenic
phosphorus—and fed him on raw carrots : they pretended to
be eliminating excess salt from his body. They might a

well have beaten him and have had done with it ; when he
went south for the winter to Bandol he was near death.

Lawrence and Frieda moved into the Villa Beau Soleil in
October.

> We are installed in this commonplace little bourgeois house,
> that was made by a femme entre-tenue and is her ideal : awful.
> But it is right on the edge of the sea ; I can lie and look out
> through the open doors at the sun on the water, and the foam
> against the islands, so I like it all right.

His old friends the Brewsters were living close by, and a
cat walked in on them to play something of the rôle that
had been played by Pipsey the dog at the Del Monte Ranch.

> We've got a cat—a young yellow " marmalade " cat with a
> white breast, who simply forced himself on us. He is very
> nice, but I never knew a French cat before—sang-froid, will of
> his own, *aimable*, but wasting no emotion. I like him very
> much, but I don't love him—which is perhaps as it should be.
> He simply abandoned his French home, and howled like a lion
> on the terrace till I let him live here—he's about eight months,
> I suppose. . . .

This simple relationship became complicated when Madame
Douillet of the hotel in Bandol where they'd spent the
previous winter sent a gift of—

> two goldfish, or one gold and one silver . . . they are the
> bane of the cat's life, for he thinks they are demons or
> phantasmagoria as they go round and gleam and become
> unnaturally huge in the glass.

But the cat all too soon recognised that a fish was a fish
even in a glass bowl and found itself in Lawrence's bad
books.

> The cat made an attack on the goldfish to-day, and a few
> small brilliant gold scales are floating loose. I spanked him
> and he looked like a Chinese demon. Now he's trying to
> make up to me—but I'm cold. . . .

D.H.L.—6

The disease slowly beat him down. First he had to give in and become bedridden. Then he had to face the beastliness of moving into a sanatorium—the Ad Astra at Vence among the inland hills. He went there to die in January 1930, but he wouldn't admit it : he went there to get well enough to travel again, to stand the long sea voyage to Mexico, to go back to the ranch. After a terrible fight he died on 2nd March ; there was little of him mortal left—he had lost weight rapidly for six months, and for the month before he died had enjoyed little sleep and much pain, yet he slipped away inch by inch. It would have been so easy just to collapse, turn his face to the wall and go, but his proud delight in life kept him from going. Each day brought with it new experience, new richness. It has been said that he longed for death, that he lived with his face to the dark, that he loved death as an escape from the intellect and its problems. But when his disease struck him in Oaxaca he was given two years to die in, and he lived for five. And even after the wicked salt-cranks had shattered him with their arsenic and phosphorus rubbish he fought on for six agonising months. He died true to his creed :

> For man, the vast marvel is to be alive. For man, as for flower and beast and bird, the supreme triumph is to be most vividly, most perfectly alive. Whatever the unborn and the dead may know, they cannot know the beauty, the marvel of being alive in the flesh. The dead may look after the afterwards. But the magnificent here and now of life in the flesh is ours, and ours alone, and ours only for a time. We ought to dance with rapture that we should be alive and in the flesh, and part of the living, incarnate cosmos. I am part of the sun as my eye is part of me. That I am part of the earth my feet know perfectly, and my blood is part of the sea. . . .

## CHAPTER VII

THE dominating factor in any assessment of Lawrence as a writer is that he was a religious leader first, and a writer second. His literary work was, after *The White Peacock* and *The Trespasser*, merely a means to an end—the end being the vulgarisation of the message which he felt it was his life's work to spread. An æsthetic approach to his work is therefore something of an absurdity ; it should rightly be left to those *fin-de-siècle* critics who used to gabble away about the drama of the mass, and so on. For most of his life Lawrence looked on writing as a method of expressing what are in fact religious intuitions, his novels are intended as moralities showing the consequences of living with or without the light of his beliefs. His short stories, however, are not so purely didactic—they can be regarded as holidays on which he allowed his interest in character free play. But the serious intention is never very far off, and dogma is never wholly forgotten. What they are certainly not is " works of art " in the sense in which Katharine Mansfield's Russian pastiches are works of art. Lawrence was hostile to the whole business of a self-conscious attempt to create a work of art, and so far as style went was content to arrive at the most direct and personal communication he could achieve. It is notable in the cases of most novelists or poets who have attempted to contribute to political or religious thought, that they have their artistic idiom and their solemn practical idiom. Lawrence writes an essay intended for the Educational Supplement of *The Times* in exactly the same style in which he writes a novel or a short story. It was not possible for him to be a sobersides for the Supplement, a plain speaker for a popular Sunday paper, and a simon-pure artist when it came to creative art, feeling for the word or the phrase. The critical difference is in length, nothing else.

There is, however, a good deal of artistry in Lawrence's writing, even if it was not produced by the sort of sentence and paragraph carpentry resorted to by the ordinarily artistic writer—of the type for which Proust or Conrad might serve as an example. Lawrence prepared himself for writing as Blake prepared himself for drawing, by completing the thing in the imagination—then the story or novel was written down without further self-criticism until it existed as a whole. Then it was considered as a whole rather than submitted to analysis, and if the total effect was bad, rejected. An entirely new version would then be hammered out to stand or fall by its total effect. The internal artistic or æsthetic effects were arrived at intuitively, much as a horse or cat achieves beautiful movement by doing what it wishes to do in what is to it the obvious way. So far as visual imagery is concerned Lawrence achieves as much beauty in his letters as he does anywhere else in his writing :

> There is a pheasant comes and lies by the wall under the gooseberry bushes, for shelter. He is so cold, he hardly notices us. We plan to catch him by throwing over him the netted hammock. But for the sake of his green head and his long pointed feathers, I cannot. We thought we should catch him and send him to you to eat. But when I look at him, so clear as he is and formal on the snow, I am bound to respect a thing which attains to so much perfection of grace and bearing.
>
> We have got spring coming in already. I have found a handful of the little wild narcissus, with the yellow centres and a few sweet violets, and a few purplish crimson anemone with dark centres. And one can drift about all afternoon in the boat, getting shell-fish from off the rocks under water, with

a long split cane. You know that warm, drowsy, uneasy feel of spring, when scents rouse up. It's already here. And the lizards are whipping about on the rocks, like a sudden flicking of a dried grass blade. . . .

When running out to the greater length of an article or story Lawrence added to the direct, surface appeal of the imagery by allowing the natural rhythms of spoken English full play.

> She was fortunate. Weeks went by, and though the dawn was sometimes clouded, and afternoon was sometimes grey, never a day passed sunless, and most days, winter though it was, streamed radiant. The thin little wild crocuses came up mauve and striped, the wild narcissi hung their winter stars. (*Sun.*)

There is a natural emphasis every five words or so, and the rhythm is as steady as a heart-beat. All Lawrence's stories can be read aloud very effectively, and some gain enormously by being heard rather than read. The rhythms, of course, match the growth of the story—or rather accord with the teller's excitement and mood. *The Man Who Loved Islands* is fascinating from this point of view ; the slowly beating, treacly movement of the passages describing the doomed man's dream world contrasts with the sharp drum taps of those describing the killing reality that has him by the feet. On the first island :

> Followed summer, and the cowslips gone, the wild roses faintly fragrant through the haze. There was a field of hay, the foxgloves stood looking down. In a little cove, the sun was on the pale granite where you bathed, and the shadow was in the rocks. Before the mist came stealing, and you went home through the ripening oats, the glare of the sea fading from the high air as the fog-horn started to moo on the other island. And then the sea fog went, it was autumn, the oat-sheaves lying prone, the great moon, another island rose golden out of the sea, and rising higher, the world of the sea was white.

And on the second island :

> . . . The sea, and the spume and the weather, had washed them
> all out, washed them out so there was only the sound of the
> sea itself, its own ghost, myriad voiced, communing and
> plotting and shouting all winter long.  And only the smell of
> the sea, with a few bristly bushes of gorse and coarse tufts of
> heather, among the grey, pellucid rocks, in the grey, more
> pellucid air.  The coldness, the greyness, even the soft, creeping
> fog of the sea, and the islet of rock humped up in it all, like the
> last point in space.

It is worth, perhaps, pausing in the middle of this comparison to digress into the matter of punctuation : an attempt
to parse these sentences in orthodox fashion is futile, and the
punctuation is correspondingly alien to the textbooks.  It is
breath punctuation, and under its extremely flexible rules
a comma merely indicates a less important pause than a
full-stop.  In the following passage, from the third island,
the word groupings themselves are shorter, and the rhythm
has been made more abrupt by the frequent substitution of
full-stops for commas.

> The dark days of winter drew on.  Sometimes there was no
> real day at all.  He felt ill, as if he were dissolving, as if dis-
> solution had already set in inside him.  Everything was twilight
> outside, and in his mind and soul.  Once, when he went to
> the door, he saw black heads of men swimming in his bay.
> For some moments he swooned unconscious.  It was the shock,
> the horror of unexpected human approach.  The horror in the
> twilight.  And not till the shock had undermined him and left
> him disembodied, did he realize that the black heads were seals
> swimming in.  A sick relief came over him.  But he was barely
> conscious after the shock.  Later on, he sat and wept with
> gratitude, because they were not men.  But he never realised
> that he wept.  He was too dim.  Like some strange ethereal
> animal, he no longer realised what he was doing.

Finally, short words, short word groups, and repetitions
bang the trap shut :

> The days were beginning to lengthen.  All winter the weather
> had been comparatively mild, but with much rain, much rain.
> He had forgotten the sun.  Suddenly however the air was very
> cold, and he began to shiver.  A fear came over him.  The sky
> was level and grey, and never a star appeared at night.  It was
> very cold.  More birds began to arrive.  The island was
> freezing.  With trembling hands he made a fire in his grate.
> The cold frightened him.
> And now it continued day after day, a dull deathly cold.
> Occasional crumblings of snow were in the air.  The days were
> greyly longer, but no change in the cold.  Frozen grey daylight.
> The birds passed away, flying away.  Some he saw lying
> frozen.  It was as if all life were drawing away, contracting
> away from the north, contracting southwards. . . .

The grammarian may well ask what sort of a sentence
" Frozen grey daylight " may be and what it is doing all
on its own.  Of course it is not doing anything on its own ;
it is taking its place in the sound pattern, which has as its
theme in the passage quoted above :  " The days were
beginning to lengthen."  In the second paragraph the theme
is restated as " The days were greyly longer."  The key
sound in the passage is set by the word "day" which is echoed
in " much rain, much rain, level and grey, day after day,
days were greyly, passed away, flying away, drawing
away, contracting away " ;  and these ay-ay sounds are
contrasted with the sharper five-times-repeated sound *cold*.

Another kind of effect is created by contrasting textures ;
particularly a rich descriptive texture contrasted with thin,
eviscerated, colloquial speech.  At the beginning of *Sun* the
feeble character of Juliet's husband is established with great
economy and certainly by such a contrast :

The ship sailed at midnight.  And for two hours her husband stayed with her, while the child was put to bed, and the passengers came on board.  It was a black night, the Hudson swayed with heavy blackness, shaken over with spilled dribbles of light.  She leaned on the rail, and looking down thought : This is the sea ; it is deeper than one imagines, and fuller of memories.  At that moment the sea seemed to heave like the serpent of chaos that has lived for ever.

" These partings are no good, you know," her husband was saying, at her side.  " They're no good.  I don't like them."

Perhaps the greatest merit of Lawrence's descriptive writing is that it is integrated.  His own overmastering sense of unity prevents him from dealing with the scene, the people, the animals, the things, thoughts, and action in separate departments.  There is never a divorce between the setting and the people, the action does not take place against a backdrop ; the people are part of the scene, and the action is the scene's vitality.  With many writers, particularly writers like Hudson, descriptive writing is so disintegrated that one gets an almost visual impression, as if one were watching the ground-glass plate at the back of an old-fashioned camera while the focus was being changed. When the landscape or the setting comes up sharp and clear, the birds, animals or men in front of it vanish ; when the living creatures are sharply defined the setting fogs, melts, or even vanishes entirely.  A really disintegrated writer holds his characters suspended before one on their introduction while an identity card is filled in, they are not offered visually a second time—the ticket takes their place on all subsequent occasions.  Lawrence probably learnt to avoid this vice from Hardy : although the stiff openings of Hardy's novels are perfect examples of disintegrated writing, once he gets deep into a book, and it begins to run, there is a

perfect balance of visual image, thought and action. It is
impossible to read the last two chapters of *Jude the Obscure*
without thinking of Lawrence's technique ; Arabella's
decisions, visual impressions and actions are a dynamic
whole, and Jude's death is part of the flow of events which
make Christminster. This interweaving is perhaps seen best
in the stories of Lawrence's later years, *The Captain's Doll,
St. Mawr* or *The Virgin and the Gipsy*, but Hardy's influence
is more obvious in the earlier stories : the following passage
which begins the story called *Odour of Chrysanthemums*, for
instance, is manifestly written under Hardy's influence :

> The small locomotive engine, Number 4, came clanking,
> stumbling down from Selston with seven full wagons. It
> appeared round the corner with loud threats of speed, but the
> colt that it startled from among the gorse, which still flickered
> indistinctly in the raw afternoon, outdistanced it at a canter.
> A woman, walking up the railway line to Underwood, drew
> back into the hedge, held her basket aside, and watched the
> footplate of the engine advancing. The trucks thumped heavily
> past, one by one, with slow inevitable movement as she stood
> insignificantly trapped between the jolting black wagons and
> the hedge ; then they curved away towards the coppice where
> the withered oak leaves dropped noiselessly, while the birds,
> pulling at the scarlet hips beside the track, made off into the
> dusk that had already crept into the spinney. In the open, the
> smoke from the engine sank and cleaved to the rough grass.
> The fields were dreary and forsaken, and in the marshy strip
> that led to the whimsey, a reedy pit pond, the fowls had already
> abandoned their run among the alders, to roost in the tarred
> fowl house. The pit bank loomed up beyond the pond, flames
> like red sores licking up its ashy sides, in the afternoon's stagnant
> light. Just beyond rose the tapering chimneys and the clumsy
> black headstocks of Brinsley Colliery. The two wheels were
> spinning fast up against the sky, and the winding engine rapped
> out its little spasms. The miners were being turned up.

Faced with such material it is difficult to maintain the

theory that Lawrence did not write as a self-conscious artist ;
but there seems in the end no doubt that his working method
excluded phrase polishing. The polishing was all done in
the preliminary phase of concentration, while the thing
was being given reality for the inner eye, then when it was
completed it was rushed on to paper. The imaginative,
gestative period was not one of sober reflection, of rational
thinking ; it was more playing and playing with the idea
and various aspects of it, until suddenly in an intense gleam
the thing was seen as a whole—the actual writing being
done under the spell of the same intense feeling. Lawrence
called it " tapping the subconscious," which as a method
is all very well up to a point.

The point is somewhere round about four or five days'
work—it is possible to maintain a passion, or to keep in
touch with the same area of the unconscious for some such
comparatively short time. A short story can be written
well within its bounds, a novel cannot. That is the principal
reason why Lawrence's short stories are so much better than
his novels. The first bores in an oilfield blow gushers into
the air, the later ones have to go on the pump and drag
the oil up out of the ground—in the end the oil-bearing
subsoil gives so meanly that oil won't seep into the shaft
bottoms fast enough to feed the pumps. Once a novel has
been started it has to go on—the laws of the book-trade are
inexorable—for seventy thousand words at least, preferably
for ninety thousand. Now and then Lawrence would tap
his subconscious and find it yielding grudgingly indeed.
While he was writing *Kangaroo* he tapped Chapter XII, that
superb gusher " The Nightmare," which flings up his
wartime experiences in fifty-three superb pages, but in
Chapter XIII the stream fades and dies out. As it dies

Lawrence tries hard to prime it with the Sermon on the Mount, but the flow dies dead and he flatly chucks in his hand.

> After all this terrific upheaval, Richard Lovat at last gave it up, and went to sleep. A man must even know how to give up his own earnestness when its hour is over, and not bother about anything any more, when he's bothered enough.

Chapter XIV is another desperate attempt to get the pump flowing again, this time a few back numbers of the *Sydney Bulletin* are shredded up and fed in for priming—among other cuttings a horse mange recipe contributed by somebody using the pseudonym " Cellu Lloyd." But the *Sydney Bulletin* proves to be no more effective than the Sermon on the Mount. Lawrence passes on to Chapter XV, after calling Chapter XIV with brutal frankness " Bits," and tries having a chat with the reader while he gives the characters a shake—it is rather like a housewife chatting with a neighbour while she hangs her washing in the back yard.

> Chapter follows chapter, and nothing doing. But man is a thought adventurer, and his falls into the Charybdis of ointment, and his shipwrecks on the rock of ages, and his kisses across chasms, and his silhouette on a minaret : surely these are as thrilling as most things.
> To be brief, there was a Harriet, a Kangaroo, a Jack, a Jaz, and a Vicky, let alone a number of mere Australians. But you know as well as I do that Harriet is quite happy rubbing her hair with hair wash and brushing it over her forehead . . . and Kangaroo has just got a very serious brief, with thousands and thousands of pounds at stake in it. Of course he is fully occupied keeping them at stake, till some of them wander into his pocket. And Jack and Vicky have gone down to her father's for the week-end, and he's out fishing . . . while she's trotting over on a pony to have a look at an old sweetheart. . . . And Jaz is arguing with a man about freight rates. And

all the scattered Australians are just having a bet on something or other. So what's wrong with Richard's climbing a mental minaret or two in the interim ? . . . We can't be at a stretch of tension all the time, like the E string on a fiddle. If you don't like the novel, don't read it. If the pudding doesn't please you, leave it, leave it. I don't mind your saucy plate, I know too well that you can bring an ass to water, etc.

Once the intense creative mood is gone there is nothing left, it is hit or miss. Sometimes, too, the intense creative urge does not come—a mood of excitement, of surface excitation, can be mistaken for it and the writing comes not from the subconscious but from a surface area of undigested impressions. The extraordinarily feeble muddle called *The Last Laugh* is obviously the result of such a mistake ; *Glad Ghosts* is another such gabble. Lawrence affected a rough language that was in its intention a gesture against " art for art's sake " writing, and this made it easy for him to miss the essential feebleness of the weak, slangy writing he did in his bogus creative excitements—and he had in any case hardly any critical faculty where his own work was concerned. He had indeed not much interest in it once it was through the creative process, he was slovenly at correcting his proofs, and let gross errors stand in his printed work through sheer indifference to fine points. Consequently a dead passage, such as that we have quoted from *Kangaroo*, or such as the opening paragraph of *Glad Ghosts*, had as good a chance of survival as his best work.

I knew Carlotta Fell in the early days before the war. Then she was escaping into art, and was just " Fell." That was at our famous but uninspired school of art, the Thwaite, where I myself was diligently murdering my talent. At the Thwaite they always gave Carlotta the still life prizes. She accepted them calmly, as one of our conquerors, but the rest of the students felt vicious about it. They called it buttering the laurels, because Carlotta was Hon., and her father a well-known peer. . . .

It is obvious that in this passage Lawrence is getting nowhere near the subconscious, he is just mining his random odds and ends of gossip—changing the names is as far as the digestion and universalisation of the creative process has gone.

Of Lawrence's forty-nine short stories fourteen can be written down as failures, and ten of these failures are among the last twenty stories he wrote. But if the risks of the hit-or-miss process apparently tended to increase as time went on, the successes were greater—good as the early stories were they do not approach *Sun, The Man Who Loved Islands, The Escaped Cock* (or *The Man Who Died*) and *The Virgin and the Gipsy*—but the failures intensify from stumbles to honest prattfalls.

The earliest complete failure is *A Fragment of Stained Glass*, but though it is a complete failure it is merely a dull story ; *Things*, the last failure, is not even that, merely a fuzzy anecdote. The two have, however, one thing in common, they represent attempts on Lawrence's part to move outside the realm of his personal experience. In a *Fragment of Stained Glass* Lawrence attempts to put himself into the skin of a medieval villein, and in *Things* he attempts to put on an American personality. The extent of the failure of the latter story can be judged by comparing it with Hemingway's *Mr. and Mrs. Elliot*, an American treatment of an identical theme. Hemingway's story is visually barren, and Lawrence's much stronger in that respect ; but Hemingway knows the essence of being an expatriate American—Lawrence can only produce a hybrid by mating his English knowledge of the expatriate situation with his gossip knowledge of the Brewsters and his other American acquaintances. One may add that it is ill-natured gossip about the Brewsters, just as *England, My England* is ill-natured gossip about other friends who gave him friendship and a comfortable home at one of his critical periods. *England, My England* possibly fails for that reason alone ; it is a gesture of repudiation of a hateful obligation, and when Lawrence takes his central figure out and kills him in a battle in France he is doing something which has as little to do with literature as making wax dolls and sticking pins into them has to do with sculpture. Like the real malicious village gossip Lawrence is revenging himself, and the result is poisonous. *Samson and Delilah* fails because it is gossip also, though it is not tinged with malice. Here Lawrence is drawing on his Cornish experience too soon, before it is digested, and the result is a trivial anecdote. *Tickets, Please !* is just as trivial so far as the story is concerned, but Lawrence fully understands the life behind it and his Nottingham experiences enable him to make the thing pyschologically rich. Later, when Lawrence had digested his Cornish experience, his understanding of that iron and sea-battered country enabled him to create the magic dream-Hebrides of *The Man Who Loved Islands*; that is written from the depths of his spirit, and *Samson and Delilah* is not. When he wrote it Cornwall had not sunk deep enough into him.

Another of the early failures is *The Ladybird*, a story which makes an extraordinary contrast with *The Fox*—written almost immediately after it. The theme is the same in both stories, an intruder from another world breaking into an established union. In *The Ladybird* it is a Polish aristocrat who causes the revision of the relationship between the

daughter of a peer and her husband—a politician's son. T
basis of the characterisation is Lawrence's extremely superficial knowledge of Lady Cynthia Asquith and her husband,
and the story can again be put in the category of gossip,
though it is irresponsible rather than malicious. The political
and country-house background from which they sprang is
described in flat insensitive language that leaves the couple
entirely unrealised :

> And she, Lady Beveridge, had for years as much influence
> on the tone of English politics as any individual alive. The
> close friend of the real leaders in the House of Lords and in
> the Cabinet, she was content that the men should act, so long
> as they breathed from her as from the rose of life the pure
> fragrance of truth and genuine love. . . .

Even those who can give their unreserved admiration for
the political and social lives of Campbell-Bannerman and
Asquith cannot think of the function of political hostesses in
quite those terms. The foundation of the story is in fact
poppycock. But in *The Fox* the intruder is a farmer's
grandson who has become an outsider by running off to
Canada, and the united pair are two lower-middle-class girls
running a poultry farm ; Lawrence knows that world inside
out, from psychological motive down to poultry ailments.
The foundation is not poppycock, but his own vividly felt
experience at Haggs Farm during his boyhood and adolescence. He has really seen that with his inward eye ; the
political country-house world to which Edward Marsh
introduced him dazzled him, and all he seemed able to notice
was the small splash he made in it.

Perhaps it is because Lawrence wrote only one more
story, *The Virgin and the Gipsy*, drawing directly on that
section of his experience that the proportion of failures to

successes increases after *The Fox*. *Two Blue Birds*, though dressed up to suggest that it has something to say about marriage, is nothing more than writer's shop ; *Smile* is a kick in the pants for one old friend at the bier of another ; *The Last Laugh* is an elaborate Hampstead-bohemian practical joke into which Lawrence has slapped a caricature of Dorothy Brett to save himself the trouble of inventing a central character ; *In Love* shows three young Art-School-and-Ibsen persons pretending to be the sort of people who lived at Haggs Farm ; *Glad Ghosts* is another poorly con-structed anecdote pivoting on a caricature of Dorothy Brett ; *The Lovely Lady* is a careless theft from Aldous Huxley ; *Rawdon's Roof* and *The Blue Moccasins* would be tolerable only if told over a good lunch about people one knew—as literature they are inexcusable. All these failures show the same poverty of visual imagery, and in all of them the characters suffer from the same lack of realised background —they do not have an origin in any section of any com-munity. When he wrote them Lawrence was drawing from the shallow forefront of his mind, but the dazzle of excite-ment was indistinguishable from the deep Shamanesque intoxication of his truly creative moods.

There is, however, one exception among the ranks of the undoubted failures, the splendidly textured Mexican story called *The Woman Who Rode Away*, which is about a woman who really does come from America, and about Indians who really exist on the soil of Mexico. But the whole thing is, really, a forgery. Lawrence hoped to find a living religion among the Indians, but he in fact found the dead carcass of a religion—dead to the uttermost, existing only as a formal gesture for the benefit of the American tourists, as a sort of proof that the reservation life was genuine. Lawrence found that it was anything but genuine really, but made a terrible fight to make it come alive for himself. *The Woman Who Rode Away*, like *The Plumed Serpent*, is wishful thinking, a determined attempt to create a compensation for a bitter disappointment—to write the disappointment out of reality. The true mood to which Mexico moved Lawrence is given in the fragment of the unfinished novel *The Flying Fish*, published posthumously in the volume called *Phœnix*. In *The Woman Who Rode Away* he forces himself to the expression of an experience that he did not have, and the validity of which he did not concede. An artist who had not shared St. Teresa's mystical experience could successfully express it if he looked towards God through the same casement ; but not believing God to be visible from that point, or to exist at all, he certainly could not. Lawrence, believing in the life of the body as the supreme human fulfilment, was being entirely untrue to his belief in making his white woman find the way to fulfilment by accepting death at the hands of the Indians. The effect is as dead as the religious work of the smart rationalist painters of the eighteenth century who tried to counterfeit mysticism with the contortions of eroticism. Lawrence's bad work is usually shallow, this story is actually corrupt.

The argument that Lawrence wrote badly when he moved outside the area of his personal experience is superficially disposed of by the content of two of the earliest among the best short stories, *The Prussian Officer* and *The Thorn in the Flesh*. It is perfectly true that Lawrence was never a German in the German Army, but when he wrote the stories he was in a special relationship—of some delicacy—to a German Field Officer, and at the disadvantage of being his social inferior. Lawrence has used this situation to enable himself to picture the situation of a German in the even worse position of a social inferior really in the Prussian Officer' power. In *The Thorn in the Flesh* his father-in-law actually appears, a careful portrait with his correct title. Both stories differ essentially, however, from the gossip type in which Lawrence uses undigested experience in an immediate way. Lawrence here uses his experience as a key to unlock some German mysteries, by considering what has happened to him he arrives at something generally true about Germans. Since the introduction of a particularly narrow type of Chauvinism as part of the right-wing political apparatus, it has become fashionable to pretend that national characteristics are not real—but left-wing intellectual humbug can as safely be disregarded as the right-wing kind and it is true that generalisations about the German or any other national character are possible and can be sound. Lawrence was not taken in by the surface glitter of the German military machine, the militarised state, and immediately penetrated to the truth that it was a national expression of what psychologists call *angst*—an anxiety state—and that its normal mode was tension rather than discipline and order. Both *The Prussian Officer* and *The Thorn in the Flesh* are about outbursts of a particularly German kind of hysterical violence produced by this intolerable everyday tension—they are valuable studies of the state of mind which led the Germans into their two last wars, and doomed them to defeat in them. Things were different in 1870 because the French then were nearly as hysterical about power, and force, and so on, but rather more exhausted by some two hundred years of it, and they collapsed before Germany was overtaken by one of her self-destroying berserk moods. Lawrence was just as perceptive about the false peace that follows those moods ; the wallow in failure and disaster which seem to the Germans the height of luxury compared with the tension of success, and the terrible burden of victory. *The Captain's Doll* and *The Border Line* deal with the atmosphere of Germany in the dead years after 1919, though the terrible reality of the German mood is used in both stories as a background to statements about certain aspects of the English character and not as the main theme. It might perhaps be more accurate to say that in the stories the English character is being brought out by exploiting its points of difference with the German. Lawrence again uses his private experience with Frieda as the way into the story, but in the creative process the privacy of the experience is purged out. It is, at first sight, odd that Hepburn in *The Captain's Doll* should be so typical an Englishman, and so typical of the educated governing class, after Lawrence's complete failure to create such a character in *The Ladybird*, written not long before. But, while he had no way into Cynthia Asquith's world, he could enter it through the Army of Occupation's contact with Germany and the Germans. *The Border Line* is perhaps a less successful story, because the characters have been taken much further as symbols than is usual with Lawrence : experience has been generalised nearly to the point of abstraction, and the characters are nearly as much ideas as they are people. The German woman who lets her flesh-and-blood second husband die for the love of the ghost of the first husband—whose flesh and blood were rather repulsive to her in life—is Germania rather than a woman. One has sometimes a certain reluctance to interpret a story to this extent, but in this case Lawrence wrote his own interpretation, or rather wrote *A Letter from Germany* which is the abstract form of

the story. Comparison of the two puts this beyond doubt
and throws some considerable light on Lawrence as a writer :

It is a miserable journey from Paris to Nancy, through that
Marne country, where the country still seems to have had the
soul blasted out of it, though the dreary fields are ploughed
and level, and the pale wire trees stand up. But it is all void
and null. And in the villages, the smashed houses in the street
rows, like rotten teeth between good teeth.

(*A Letter from Germany.*)

As she looked unseeing out of the carriage window, suddenly,
with a jolt, the wintry landscape realised itself into her
consciousness. The flat, grey, wintry landscape, ploughed
fields of greyish earth that looked as if they were compounded
of the clay of dead men. Pallid, stark, thin trees stood like
wire beside straight, abstract roads. A ruined farm between a
few more trees. And a dismal village filed past, with smashed
houses like rotten teeth between the straight rows of the village
street.

With sudden horror she realised she must be in the Marne
country, the ghastly Marne country, century after century
digging the corpses of frustrated men into its soil. The border
country where the Latin races and the Germanic neutralise
one another into horrid ash.

(*The Border Line.*)

It was a cold, wintry night, but she wanted to go out after
dinner to see the Minster. She remembered it all so well, in
that other life.

The wind blew icily in the street. The town seemed empty,
as if its spirit had left it. The few squat, hefty foot-passenger
were all talking the harsh Alsatian German. Shop signs were
in French, often with a little concession to German underneath.
And the shops were full of goods, glutted with goods from the
once-German factories of Mulhausen and other cities.

(*The Border Line.*)

You come to Strasburg, and the people still talk Alsatian

German, as ever, in spite of French shop signs. The place feels dead. And full of cotton goods, white goods, from Mulhausen, from the factories that once were German. Such cheap white cotton goods, in a glut.

(*A Letter from Germany.*)

The Cathedral front rearing up high and flat and fanciful, a sort of darkness in the dark, with round rose windows and long, long prisons of stone. Queer, that men should have ever wanted. to put stone upon fanciful stone to such a height, without having it fall down. The Gothic ! I was always glad when my card castle fell. But these Goths and Alemans seemed to have a craze for peaky heights.

(*A Letter from Germany.*)

She remembered the little street, the old, overhanging houses with black timbers and high gables. And like a great ghost, a reddish flush in its darkness, the uncanny cathedral breasting the oncomer, standing gigantic, looking down in darkness out of darkness, on the pygmy humanness of the city. It was built of reddish stone, that had a flush in the night, like dark flesh. And vast, an incomprehensibly tall, strange thing, it looked down out of the night. The great rose window, poised high, seemed like a breast of the vast Thing, and prisms and needles of stone shot up, as if it were plumage, dimly, half visible in heaven. . . . [A paragraph about the demonish menace of the cathedral.]

Mystery and dim, ancient fear came over the woman's soul. The cathedral looked so strange and demonish heathen. And an ancient indomitable blood seemed to stir in it. It stood there like some vast silent beast with teeth of stone, waiting, and wondering when to stoop against this pallid humanity.

(*The Border Line.*)

The letter and the story begin to diverge in form and accent at this point of the cathedral : so far as the letter is concerned it does not amount to much ; in the story it is an outpost of the northern Germanic spirit in Latin territory, and the demonish menace which invests it is the new death

spirit which has gripped Germany.   This death spirit is
introduced immediately after the image of the cathedral has
been developed ;  a man is standing waiting for the heroine
of the story in its black shadow, and just as she realises that
he is waiting for her she also realises that he is a ghost.   The
woman and the ghost walk through the town, but he leaves
her after a time to go back to her living husband ;  he cannot
claim her here—on this side of the river.

The river barrier is given equal force in the story and the
letter :

> The Rhine is still the Rhine, the great divider.   You feel
> it as you cross.   The flat, frozen watery places.   Then the cold
> and curving river.   Then the other side, seeming so cold, so
> empty, so frozen, so forsaken.   The train stands and steams
> fiercely.   Then it draws through the flat Rhine plain, past
> frozen pools of black flood water, and frozen fields, in the
> emptiness of this bit of occupied territory.
>
> Immediately you are over the Rhine, the spirit of the place has
> changed.   There is no more attempt at the bluff of geniality. . . .
> The fields are vacant.   There seems nobody in the world.
>
> *(A Letter from Germany.)*


> . . . She waited while the hot train steamed and hissed,
> arrested at the perfect neutral point of the new border line, just
> across the line.
>
> And at last a little sun came out, and the train silently drew
> away, nervously, from the neutrality.
>
> In the great flat field of the Rhine plain, the shallow flood
> water was frozen, the furrows ran straight towards nowhere,
> the air seemed frozen too, but the earth felt strong and barbaric,
> it seemed to vibrate, with its straight furrows, in a deep savage
> undertone.   There was a frozen, savage thrill in the air also,
> something wild and unsubdued, pre-Roman.
>
> This part of the Rhine valley, even on the right bank in
> Germany, was occupied by the French ;  hence the curious
> vacancy, the suspense, as if no men lived there, but some spirit

was watching, watching over the vast, empty, straight furrowed
fields and the water meadows.   Stillness, emptiness, suspense,
and a sense of something still impending.

(*The Border Line.*)

The letter then goes on into an analysis of the nature of
this something, in abstract terms ; the story carries the idea
on in purely personal terms.   The ghost is waiting here, and
here in Germany he can take actual physical possession of
his wife—and with the cold chill of his nothingness destroy
her husband.   There is an extraordinarily deft handling of
detail in the business of the increasing reality of the ghost ;
when he first appears in the shadow of the cathedral he is
in his officer's cap, his face shadowy under it, and when he
comes walking out of the German pinewoods his face is
unshaded, his head bare—he is a dead man who can outface
the living.   And as the ghost grows in the devotion and
passion of the woman her living husband dwindles, and dies
while her love of death is being consummated.   Without
*A Letter from Germany* the friendly critic would be on an
equal footing with the hostile one, one merely saying black
where the other says white.   The hostile critic following the
easy line marked out by E. T. and Middleton Murry holds
up *The Border Line* as typical of Lawrence's writing from
his neurosis—the woman wedded to death is simply Lawrence longing for the dark of the womb.   But it seems
remarkable that Lawrence writing a letter should be able to
think about Germany, while Lawrence writing a story
should just go softly slopping into his own neurosis.

Germany, this bit of Germany, is very different from what
it was two and a half years ago, when I was here.   Then it
was still open to Europe.   Then it still looked to Western
Europe for a re-union, for a sort of reconciliation.   Now that

is over. The inevitable, mysterious barrier has fallen again, and the great leaning of the Germanic spirit is once more Eastwards, towards Russia, towards Tartary. The strange vortex of Tartary has become the positive centre again, the positivity of western Europe is broken. The positivity of our civilisation has broken. The influences that come, come invisibly out of Tartary. So that all Germany reads *Beasts, Men and Gods* with a kind of fascination. Returning again to the fascination of the destructive East, that produced Attila. . . . And it all looks as if the years were wheeling swiftly backwards, no more onwards. Like a spring that is broken, and whirls swiftly back, so time seems to be whirling with mysterious swiftness to a sort of death. Whirling to the ghost of the Middle Ages of Germany, then to the Roman days, then to the days of the silent forest, and the dangerous lurking barbarians.

And Lawrence predicts disaster for Europe from this reversal. It is terribly easy to mock at Lawrence for his lack of restraint, and for his emotionalism : the mind tempered in the classical school knows that furrows in a half-flooded field do not vibrate, that a savage thrill cannot be felt in the air of any place, and that such things cannot have any place in a rational chain of thought that would satisfy the requirements of logic. But all the same Lawrence does in the letter and the story go to the heart of the German sickness, and sees the doom that is to come. It is worth pointing out that the time of writing was February 1924, when more logical persons were taking quite another view of the German problem, and a much less realistic one.

But right or wrong about Germany, *The Border Line* with *A Letter from Germany* shows just how Lawrence was tied to his personal experience. He is able to get into the skin of a woman, of another man, but he could only do it if they were going to have an experience which he had enjoyed—he was not an imaginative writer like Balzac, or a spider like Proust able to sit in a web of talk sucking out the richer blood of people with more active lives. His gift is to take you where he has been, see what he saw, and, to a lesser extent, feel what he felt.

This limitation of his genius is less apparent in the short stories and poems than it is in the novels; for obvious reasons, a short story must, almost inevitably, concern a selected group of people and a limited sector of experience. It will probably be a bad story if it does go beyond that scope. However, in the small scale of the short story Lawrence achieves results of real grandeur : *Love Among the Haystacks*, *The Daughters of the Vicar*, *The Shades of Spring*, *The Fox*, *The Captain's Doll*, *The Man Who Loved Islands*, *The Rocking Horse Winner* and *The Man Who Died* are among the best short stories in the English language, and one is not aware of any limitations while one is reading them.

## CHAPTER VIII

*T*HE WHITE PEACOCK, the first of Lawrence's novels, is an attempt to write a conventional novel— to make a work of art. Lawrence was not then sure enough of himself to write it as a direct expression of his ideas, and the characters do not explicitly preach the attitudes to life which they represent. Nevertheless, the essential dogma is there, and the book shows doom falling on those whose idealism forces them to be untrue to the life of the body. The corrupting idealism is largely of a pre-Raphaelite type, it is curious to see how many of the cultural references in the book are to the art and literature of that movement, so easily written off as dead and unimportant by contemporary critics. It is manifest from this book that the pre-Raphaelite movement was the strongest cultural influence working on Lawrence in his early years. The mental barriers between lovers which play such a large part in pre-Raphaelite mythology, which doom so many young persons to premature, hollow-cheeked death, play their part in *The White Peacock*. The two central figures, Lettie and George, are obviously made for each other. But she is refined, delicately minded, and well brought up, so that she finds his rough farm ways intolerable. The curse of idealism is on her, she wants a more Galahad-like figure, she wants a purer, less animal love. So she marries a well-found man with good manners, and George is left and marries a barmaid. The barmaid Meg is really the same woman as Lettie, but she is from a lower layer in the social cake, with a materialist parody of Lettie's idealism. For Meg, Galahad is a respectable

man, and all Lettie's stuff about purity and delicacy comes
out in terms of not speaking dialect, and having a maid
who eats in the kitchen. George goes to pieces and drinks
himself to physical ruin.

While George and Lettie find their doom, another pair,
Cyril and Emily, find theirs. Cyril is the narrator, a rather
disembodied presence, who wanders on the fringe of the
story, now part of it, now an objective observer. His main
special sympathy is with George, who is the strongly built
proud animal he would like to be—he is educated up out
of his class and lives in a web of intellectual difficulty and
self-criticism. And he has been educated, too, out of his
natural affinity with Emily, the feminine equivalent of
George. They drift apart, further and further. Until at the
end of the book Emily is married to a farmer, who is what
George ought to have been, and what Cyril could have
been, too. Cyril visits their farm at harvest, to see George
who is staying there and recovering from a bout of delirium
tremens.

> It was the home of the Renshaws, warm, lovable, serene.
> Emily was in perfect accord with its brownness, its shadows,
> its ease. I, as I sat on the sofa under the window, felt rejected
> by the kind room. I was distressed with a sense of ephemerality,
> of pale erratic fragility.
> Emily in her full-blooded beauty was at home. It is rare
> now to feel kinship between a room and the one who inhabits
> it, a close bond of blood relation. Emily had at last found her
> place, and had escaped from the torture of strange, complex
> modern life.

The woman's place is in the home, and the man's place
is in joyous, creative physical labour : with both in their
recognised places marriage really is as merry as a marriage
bell.

I watched the tall, square-shouldered man, leaning with deference and tenderness towards his wife as she walked calmly at his side.  She was the mistress, quiet and self-assured, he her rejoiced husband and servant.

The book ends with the two men, betrayed to death by being false to themselves, watching the life of the farm :

In the stackyard, the summer's splendid monuments of wheat and grass were reared in gold and grey.  The wheat was littered brightly round the rising stack.  The loaded wagon clanked slowly up the incline, drew near, and rode like a ship at anchor against the scotches, brushing the stack with a crisp sharp sound.  Tom climbed the ladder and stood a moment there against the sky, amid the brightness and fragrance of the golden corn, and waved his arm to his wife who was passing in the shadow of the building.  Then Arthur began to lift the sheaves to the stack, and the two men worked in an exquisite, subtle rhythm, their white sleeves, and their dark heads gleaming, moving against the mild sky and the corn.  The silence was broken only by the occasional lurch of the body of the wagon, as the teamer stepped to the front or again to the rear of the load.  Occasionally I could catch the blue glitter of the prongs of the forks.  Tom, now lifted high above the small wagon load, called to his brother some question about the stack.  The sound of his voice was strong and mellow.

The two men standing watching are looking at something just as important for Lawrence as the happy marriage : the harmony of common work and common joy which allows Arthur and Tom to achieve an exquisite, subtle rhythm is something which George and Cyril have thrown away.  Lawrence considers that they have lost, in that, something just as important as their man-to-woman relationship.  The book is more explicit about this than anything else, and Chapter VIII of Part Two, " A Poem of Friendship," is one of Lawrence's most splendid passages : it describes in vivid personal terms what he reduced to an abstraction in his essay, "Education of the People." It is the obsession behind Rananim, the recurrent theme of so much of his work :

> And between men let there be a new, spontaneous relationship, a new fidelity. Let men realise that their life lies ahead, in the dangerous wilds of advance and increase. Let them realise that they must go beyond their women, projected into a region of greater abstraction, more inhuman activity.
>
> There in these womanless regions of fight, and pure thought, and abstracted instrumentality . . . let there be again the old passion of deathless friendship between man and man. . . . Friendship should be a rare, choice, immortal thing, sacred and inviolable as marriage. Marriage and deathless friendship, both should be inviolable and sacred : two great creative passions, separate, apart, but complementary : the one pivotal, the other adventurous : the one marriage, the centre of human life ; and the other the leap ahead.
>
> Which is the last word in the education of a people.

Perhaps the weakest point in *The White Peacock* is one of the most interesting about Lawrence. Chapter II of Part Two, "A Shadow in Spring," is entirely irrelevant, a short story which has been incorporated into the book for no reason at all. But it is not only interesting because the central figure, the gamekeeper Annable, is a character who reappears as Mellors in *Lady Chatterley's Lover*, for Annable is also The Intruder, the man from another world, who plays a leading part in Lawrence's imagination. Annable, the intruder on his first appearance, has been to Cambridge, has been a clergyman, and has been married to an aristocratic person (filched whole from Marie Corelli) called Lady Crystabel, but all that is behind him : he slipped on servant's clothes, slipped away, and vanished. Lady Crystabel thinks him dead. He is free. Mellors, who most closely resembles him, is freed from working-class status by his war service, he has slipped on the clothes of an officer and vanished from his normal world too. In the crisis of their old lives these men have discarded all the conceptions which divide their mental and physical beings, and they have acquired a direct sympathy with the dynamic forces which make the sap rise and the earth turn. In the end Mellors and *The Man Who Died* are the same person. The figure of the intruder is drawn again and again, on various scales. In *The Daughters of the Vicar* he is the miner who carries off the girl from the vicarage, he is the gipsy of *The Virgin and the Gipsy*, he is Count Dionys of *The Ladybird*, the groom of *St. Mawr*, the Mexican guide of *The Princess*, and the man from Canada in *The Fox*. It is perhaps a little doubtful if the intruder is the Polish girl of *Love Among the Haystacks*, who is the same person as Lydia Lensky of *The Rainbow*; though both have many of his characteristics they are essentially feminine and the character is dependent on its physical maleness. He appears not only in *The White Peacock* and *Lady Chatterley's Lover* among the novels, but also as Hampson in *The Trespasser*, Cicio in *The Lost Girl*, Loerke in *Women in Love*, Lilly in *Aaron's Rod*, and Kangaroo in *Kangaroo*.

Where does he come from ? When Cyril, the narrator of *The White Peacock*, goes to find him he looks for him in a suitable enough setting :

> The grassy path to the churchyard was still clogged with decayed leaves. The church is abandoned. As I drew near an owl floated softly out of the black tower. Grass overgrew the threshold. I pushed open the door, grinding back a heap of fallen plaster and rubbish, and entered the place. In the twilight the pews were leaning in ghostly disorder, the prayer books dragged from their ledges, scattered on the floor in the dust and rubble torn by the mice and birds. Birds scuffled in

the darkness of the roof. I looked up. In the upward well
of the tower I could see a bell hanging. I stooped and picked
up a piece of plaster from the ragged confusion of feathers,
and broken nests and dead birds. Up into the vault overhead
I tossed pieces of plaster until one hit the bell and it tonged
out its faint remonstrance. . . .

And this act of conjuration soon conjures up Annable. It
also conjures up the rich splendours of the Romantic
Movement of a full century before. And indeed, not long
before this, Cyril and Emily, spattered with the blood of a
sheep-worrying dog they have just battered to death with
stones, have wandered hand in hand on to the Newstead
Abbey estate. It is no great distance, in fact, from Haggs
Farm to Newstead, or from The Intruder to Byron.
Lawrence remarks in his *Study of Thomas Hardy* that
" the real voluptuary is a man who is female as well as male,
and who lives according to the female side of his nature,
like Lord Byron." The remark remains true if one sub-
stitutes the phrase " Lawrence's ideal man " for " the real
voluptuary."

No new themes are to be found in the novels, they are
all concerned with restating the themes of *The White Peacock*.
The treatment of the themes changes a little, as Lawrence's
thought matures and develops, and as he comes to consider
the novel less and less important and the discussion of the
theme more and more important. The art of the novel is
still very important in *The Trespasser*, and it is less theme-
ridden than any of the others. But the hero, Siegmund, is a
life-denier, a typical Lawrence figure, doomed because he
has turned his back on the natural flow of life and been
untrue to his own nature. He is George of *The White
Peacock* over again ; but while George wanders on his

path to death over the fields and leas round Haggs Farm, Siegmund wanders between a middle-class London home and the Crimea. Lawrence pretends it is the neighbourhood of Yarmouth in the Isle of Wight, but he is so much under the spell of Tchekov that one may safely disregard the place-names which tell one that the characters are anywhere else but in Russian literature. The long death agony, in which Siegmund decides to hang himself with a trunk strap, has all the bathos of a Katherine Mansfield story—and all the inevitable weakness of writing which represents an attempt by the writer to change cultural horses in midstream. In *The Trespasser* Lawrence discards all he has learned from Hardy and Meredith, and with that all his pre-Raphaelite cultural setting ; he is trying hard to be a Russian writer, and to naturalise himself in a Wagnerian Bohemia. Lawrence is in this book ashamed of being an English provincial, just as Katherine Mansfield was ashamed of being a colonial, and, instead of attempting to enrich himself by opening his mind to alien influences, tries to stamp his provincial self into the mud and to masquerade as a Russian living in Baden. No more references to Burne-Jones and Waterhouse, no more quotations from Dante Gabriel Rossetti ; instead Siegmund whistles the juicier passages from the Wagner operas (*Die Valkure* is his favourite—and a train sings that Ho-Jo-To-Ho nonsense to him) while his mistress quotes from the original German of Goethe, Heine and Uhland. She is not content to toss such treasures as *Aus alten marchen winkt es, Hervor mit weisser Hand, Da singt es und da klingt es, Von einem Zauberland* into the flow of their talk, but she works up her own cadenzas on these bases.

> *Die grosse Blumen schmachten*, she said to herself, curiously awake and joyous. The big flowers open with black petals and

silvery ones, Siegmund.  You are the big flowers, Siegmund ;
yours is the bridegroom face, Siegmund, like a black and
glistening flesh-petalled flower, Siegmund, and it blooms in
the Zauberland, Siegmund—this is the magic land.

Happily Lawrence wrote only the one novel about it, and
for *Sons and Lovers* returned to the land which he knew by
daylight.  The gain is enormous, the papery, literary quality
of *The Trespasser* vanishes at once.  There is even a great
gain on *The White Peacock* because that, being largely about
Haggs Farm and the country, is about his world of escape.
*Sons and Lovers* is about the industrial disaster into which
he was born, and the terrible corruption of humanity which
a materialist society achieves, about what he escaped at
Haggs Farm.  The opening passage of the opening chapter
is an unsurpassed description of the last phase of the industrial
revolution, one still so close that many people have not
realised that it has taken place, in which the last technical
advances were made which took industrialism beyond the
human scale.  Lawrence describes the little village pits of his
father's boyhood, coal mines that were part of the country-
side, with their donkey-powered machinery, and then shows
them being engulfed by the new pits with their surface
engines and deep shafts, their mysterious London financing,
and their anonymous alien bosses.  The new pits are gigantic,
they blast and wither the country round them, and their
dormitory slums spread like scabs over the local villages,
annihilating them as places.  The old fellowship in work of
the free miners has gone, and in its place there is nothing but
the false unity—money hunger, really—of the Unions ;  and
as the men don't count as individuals at work they are lost
when it comes to being individuals at home.  For these
dwarfed lives Lawrence draws on his own knowledge of

D.H.L.—8

the blunted, rotten life of his father and mother, and the abundant frustrations of his own youth.

As in *The White Peacock* two pairs are shown in opposition, the mother and father against Paul Morel and Miriam. The first pair have committed the crime of being false to their true natures ; the woman will not have the man as he is but tries to force him to be something else, less virile and less free ; the man has failed to win the woman from her prejudices to an acceptance of life, he has also failed his manhood by not clearing out. They are Lettie and George over again. Paul and Miriam are Emily and Cyril, but with the difference that Miriam's fate is to be reduced to impotence by idealism this time, while Paul has Emily's luck and finds a way through into life. *Sons and Lovers* apparently introduces a new theme, about the relation of children and their parents ; but that is only apparently so. The relation of Mrs. Morel and her son is an embroidery on the text, The Sins of the Fathers ; the sin in this case being the refusal of life by the parents. Because Mrs. Morel has failed with her husband she tries to feed herself on that part of her son which belongs to his women. The point is made perfectly clear in the preface to the book Lawrence sent to Edward Garnett early in 1913, and in particular in the final passage, quoted earlier in this book. The important thing in the book is not that Mrs. Morel is Paul's mother, but that Mrs. Morel and Miriam are two aspects of the same destructive force. Paul and his father are also two versions of the same character, but once saved, and once lost. In Paul all the forces driving him towards the denial of life, to a neurotic seeking of the dark irresponsible comfort of the womb, are shown at work ; too many critics have suggested that they are shown at work with approval, and that Lawrence is trying to say that the right way to live is on the lines of Paul Morel's weakness. But everything in the book leads up to the moment when Paul, with his emotional crisis behind him, turns his back on everything his mother stands for and goes on towards life and the light.

> But no, he would not give in. Turning sharply, he walked towards the city's golden phosphorescence. His fists were shut, his mouth set fast. He would not take that direction, to the darkness, to follow her. He walked towards the faintly humming, glowing town, quickly.

*Sons and Lovers* also contains the entire body of *The Trespasser*. While Paul is maturing he has an abortive affair with a married woman called Clara Dawes (it cannot come to anything because when he enters on it he is in search of a mother, not a woman), and in the course of it they go off for a short holiday to the Lincolnshire coast. The episode forms a small part of Chapter XIII, " Baxter Dawes," pages 357 to 362 of the first edition, and in that form is perhaps an adequate atonement for the full-length novel, at least it shows how well Lawrence had learned to write about emotional transactions. The mystery is that he lacked the power to see when he reverted to the wretched *Trespasser* manner, as he did so fatally in the big two-volume novel which followed *Sons and Lovers*. This was called *The Sisters*, in draft, but was published as two novels, *The Rainbow* and *Women in Love*.

Lawrence can be caught trespassing in either volume as often as not, and *grosse blumen* flower on too many pages.

> Out of the far, far space there drifted slowly in to her a passionate, unborn yearning. " There are so many dawns that have not yet risen." It seemed as if, from over the edge of

the sea, all the unrisen dawns were appealing to her, all her unborn soul was crying for the unrisen dawns.

*(The Rainbow.)*

They continued without saying any more, walking along opposite horizons, hand in hand across the intervening space, two separate people. And he trembled as if a wind blew on to him in strong gusts out of the unseen. He was afraid. He was afraid to know he was alone. For she seemed fulfilled and separate and sufficient in her half of the world.

*(The Rainbow.)*

She traced with her hands the line of his loins and thighs, at the back, and a living fire ran through her, from him, darkly. It was a dark flood of electric passion she released from him, drew into herself. She had established a rich new circuit, a new current of passional electric energy, between the two of them, released from the darkest poles of the body and established in perfect circuit. It was a dark fire of electricity that rushed from him to her, and flooded them both with rich peace, satisfaction.

(Ursula and Birkin in *Women in Love* are at that moment
        in the parlour of The Saracen's Head at Southwell,
        Nottingham, waiting for the waiter to bring them tea.)

The passion came up in him, stroke after stroke, like the ringing of a bronze bell, so strong and unflawed, and indomitable. His knees tightened to bronze as he hung above her soft face, whose lips parted and whose eyes dilated in a strange violation. In the grasp of his hand her chin was unutterably soft and silken. He felt as strong as winter, his hands were living metal, invincible, and not to be turned aside. His heart rang like a bell clanging inside him.

He took her up in his arms. . . . But the overweening power of his body was too much for her. She relaxed again, and lay loose and soft, panting in a little delirium. And to him, she was so sweet, she was such a bliss of release, that he would have suffered a whole eternity of torture than forego one second of this pang of unsurpassable bliss.

" My god," he said to her, his face drawn and strange, transfigured, " what next ? "

(Gudrun and Gerald, in *Women in Love*.)

Edward Garnett wrote a strong protest against this Wagnerian writing when Lawrence sent him the manuscript of *The Rainbow*, and Lawrence answered him by saying that he was less interested in creating vivid scenes than in arriving at the truth about some of the physical states of being. In fact, in these two books Lawrence has embarked on the impossible business of expressing instinctive physical responses in words ; with the object of bringing about a readjustment in the relationship between men and women, that would make their approach to sex free and healthy. That is, he has set himself to the task of making men and women less self-conscious about their bodies and bodily functions by talking about them and writing about them. He is himself terribly self-conscious when he approaches the forbidden zones, he knows his readers will be, and he tries to smash his way through to frankness and ease by the literary equivalent of talking as loud and as fast as possible. In the Shaman's delirium into which he works himself by this roaring he disregards the absence of any language in the world of sensation which one enters by any purely physical activity ; so these unborn souls yearn, and gusts blow out of the unseen, and rich circuits of passional electricity crackle all over the shop.

From *The Rainbow* onwards the novels are more concerned with the physical being of the characters than with where they go, what they do, and what happens to them. The characters are not developed, they move from one physical experience to the next looking for the transforming fulfilment that will free them from their prisons of self-consciousness. What is more, the characters are not internally consistent : Lawrence is not specially interested in them as characters, he needs them to illustrate habits of mind, he just says what they think, and if it is not consistent with what they thought last time they appeared, why, who cares ? And if Lawrence gets really interested in an idea that comes up in the mind of a character, he just elbows the character aside and speaks for him—for all the world like a ventriloquist who pushes his doll to one side and, haranguing the audience, gives up all pretence at maintaining a dialogue. It is easy enough to say that Birkin of *Women in Love* is Lawrence himself, Gerald Crich—Murry, Gudrun—Katherine Mansfield, Halliday—Philip Heseltine, and so on. But that tidy systematisation breaks down, for on various occasions Lawrence speaks through them all, and if on certain occasions—such as that in which Gudrun recovers a letter of Birkin's from Halliday in the Café Royal—these identifications work, there are plenty of others on which they do not. Gudrun, for instance, is just as often Lawrence as Birkin is, and she is again just as often Frieda.

As for plot, it matches the characterisation : events follow each other rather as they do in life. It is time Tom Brangwen vanished from the story—well, we'll have a flood and wash him away. Why a flood ? Well, why not ? But suppose there hadn't been a flood . . . ? Well, that would have been another story ! This weakness is apparent in *Sons and Lovers* which would have been an altogether different book if Paul Morel's father had cleared out in Chapter II with his bundle—it would have been *Aaron's Rod*, and indeed, that is what *Aaron's Rod* is. It is not really possible to imagine an entirely different book resulting from Proust's possible failure to remember Elstir's address on the afternoon that he was to be introduced to Mlle Simonet at the painter's studio—suppose they had never met ? But that is an example of what Bergson termed, *Les questions qui ne se posent pas.* At any given moment in almost any of

Lawrence's later novels, however, it is apparent that pure chance decides what will happen next. Why is Diana Crich drowned in Chapter XIV of *Women in Love* ? Why does Somers suddenly go over his wartime experiences in Chapter XII of *Kangaroo* ? Why does Aaron go to Novara in Chapter XII of *Aaron's Rod* ? Why the murder of Jose—the Mexican-German half-breed—in Chapter VI of *The Plumed Serpent* ? There are no answers to these questions ; Lawrence's novels ignore the internal logic and order essential in a work of art. But then, of course, they were not supposed to be works of art ; they were to stand or fall by their power to make clear the nature of new relationships of man to woman, and man to man, for which he was campaigning.

As such *The Rainbow* can be written off as a total failure. It impressed the magistrates as a piece of pornography, and the most friendly reader cannot draw from it any clear picture of an ideal without recourse to Lawrence's later work. The probability is in favour of a complete mis-understanding of Lawrence's intention, springing from Chapter VIII, " The Child," in which the relations of Anna and Will Brangwen are apparently brought to perfection by his unsuccessful attempt to seduce a girl he has picked up in a Nottingham music hall. And it is just as easy to interpret the adventures of Gudrun and Ursula in both *The Rainbow* and *Women in Love* in a sense other than that intended by Lawrence ; the difference between the emotional tension which possesses Birkin and Ursula when they become lovers in Chapter XXIII, and that which possesses Gerald and Gudrun when they become lovers in Chapter XXIV, is not immediately apparent. It is possible, in fact, to doubt that there is any essential difference. Lawrence intends it to be clear that Birkin and Ursula turn towards each other and towards life, and that Gerald turns to Gudrun for shelter from his fear of death, made acute by the death of his father. To make the point he does not, however, give the first couple sexual satisfaction and the second disappointment, but gives the first pair a good night's sleep, and the woman of the second pair a bad one.    But there is good reason why Gudrun should lie awake, her lover has slipped into her father's house like a burglar and she must get him out before the household wakes in the morning ; when she has safely accomplished this, then she knows the deep satisfied sleep that Ursula has enjoyed.    That question apart, it is difficult to follow the distinction between Gerald's search for forgetfulness of his fear, and Birkin's search for a universe of dark reality, darkness, secrecy and oblivion.

*Women in Love* adds to *The Rainbow's* theme of the man-woman relationship the second theme from *The White Peacock*.    The man-man relationship of Cyril and George is repeated, the parallel to " The Poem of Friendship " chapter being " Gladiatorial," Chapter XX.    Where the two men in *The White Peacock* strip to bathe and rub each other down afterwards, in *Women in Love* Gerald and Birkin strip to wrestle, and talk afterwards.

> There were long spaces between their words.    The wrestling had some deep meaning to them—an unfinished meaning.
> " We are mentally, spiritually intimate, therefore we should be more or less physically intimate too—it is more whole."

It is ill-defined, something more complex than the simple companionship-in-work of *The White Peacock* has been conceived, but Lawrence is not really sure what.    The book ends with a less than certain note on this theme, as Ursula tries to worry it out of Birkin :

" Why aren't I enough ? " she said.   " You are enough for
me.   I don't want anybody else but you.   Why isn't it the
same with you ? "

" Having you, I can live all my life without anybody else,
any other sheer intimacy.   But to make it complete, really
happy, I wanted eternal union with a man too, another kind
of love," he said. . . .

" You can't have two kinds of love.   Why should you ! "

" It seems as if I can't," he said, " but I wanted it."

" You can't have it, because it's false, impossible," she said.

" I don't believe that," he answered.

Before closing with this difficult subject again Lawrence
turned aside to rewrite and rename *The Insurrection of Miss
Houghton*, which he had begun when he was working on
*The Rainbow*.   Whatever it may have been in its first draft
it is not a very interesting book now : if it has any obvious
affinity it is with J. B. Priestley's *Good Companions*, to which
it stands in rather the relationship of *The House with the
Green Shutters* to A. J. Cronin's *Hatter's Castle*.   It was
written in the first place as a pot-boiler, it was rewritten
rather in the spirit in which a farmer slaps new paint on to
an old cart before an auction.   *The Lost Girl* as it stands is
merely a tribute to the power of Lawrence's obsessions ;
however hard he settled down to be popular and to play
for the easy laughs he could not escape his own set pattern.
Alvina Houghton starts out on a series of picaresque
adventures, deliberately trivial adventures hung on her
father's ridiculous speculations in the drapery, coalmining
and cinema businesses, but she ends up on the quest for
fulfilment and the achievement of the full life in the body.
The book is also a tribute to Lawrence's genius ; his most
off-hand and lazy production, it remains alive and vital as
few popular novels do, and it is invested with a very real

distinction. The worst of Lawrence's books, it is bad only relatively.

The trouble with it is that Alvina's physical fulfilment lands her in an escapable physical trap. Her man Cicio is one of the children of God walking among the daughters of men, and it should be bliss for her—but instead it is the frozen poverty of the high Abruzzi. When Lawrence sat down to turn *The Insurrection of Miss Houghton* into *The Lost Girl* he was in Capri still smarting from the emotional shock he had received during a fortnight's stay at a farm by Picinisco in the Province of Caserta—he was shocked and a little frightened by its bare savagery—suppose one should be trapped in such a place ? The thought chased everything else out of his head for the moment, Alvina Houghton was to hand, so she was popped into the trap. There are no hints that she will ever find a way out, and there is no suggestion that physical fulfilment is enough to withstand the bare rock and the frozen water. The book is simply sawn off when it has reached the length of a novel, it reaches no conclusion : Alvina really is a Lost Girl.

Lawrence gets back to the unfinished question of the man-man relationship in *Aaron's Rod* and attempts to thresh it out to a final solution. Aaron Sisson at the beginning of the book shakes off a marriage relationship which has failed him, and he sets out—like Alvina Houghton—on this quest. At first he hopes to find his fulfilment in the body of some other woman who, unlike his wife, will welcome him in the pride of his manhood. But in the end he comes to realise that what he is seeking is something quite outside the possibility of the man-to-woman relationship, that is essentially a matter of the loss of self-consciousness, of self-destruction through love. Aaron is looking for something different, something which his friend Lilly—the Byronic liberated intruder of the book—attempts to define for him : there are two great life urges, love and power—there may be more.

> " And we've been trying to work ourselves, at least as individuals, from the love urge exclusively, hating the power urge, and repressing it. And now I find we've got to accept the very thing we've hated. . . . We've got to accept the power motive, accept it in deep responsibility. . . . It is a vast dark source of life and strength in us now, waiting either to issue into true action, or to burst into cataclysm. . . . Let the urge be the urge of power. . . . And of course there must be one who urges, and one who is impelled. Just as in love there is a beloved and a lover : the man is supposed to be the lover, the woman the beloved. Now, in the urge of power, it is the reverse. The woman must submit . . . yield to the deep power-soul in the individual man, and obey implicitly . . . there will be profound, profound obedience in place of this love crying, obedience to the incalculable power urge. And men must submit to the greater soul in a man, for their guidance. . . . At present, when they say they want a leader, they mean they want an instrument, like Lloyd George. A mere instrument for their use. But it's more than that . . . submission to the heroic soul in a greater man." . . . There was a long pause. Then Aaron looked up into Lilly's face. It was dark and remote-seeming. It was like a Byzantine eikon at the moment. " And whom shall I submit to ? " he said. " Your soul will tell you," replied the other.

And that is the final word. The prologue is impressive enough, but it has to be admitted that the last exchange resembles nothing so much as Victorian exchange between an anxious girl and her kindly nannie. " But how shall I know if it is Mr. Right ? " " Your heart will tell you, dear, you can't make a mistake when Mr. Right comes along."

But if *Aaron's Rod* is in the end no more than a prolonged

vanishing trick, it does contain some of Lawrence's most brilliant writing. In such passages as the Christmas scene which opens the book, the description of Novara, and of a riot in Florence, he creates fragments of the utmost beauty —fragments which possess an almost luminous clarity in opposition to the surrounding obscurity. Their beauty cannot, however, blind one to their complete lack of relation ; to the familiar lack of the cohesion and order essential to a work of art. The novel is simply a workshop in which Lawrence is hammering out new ideas.

So is *Kangaroo* ; when *Aaron's Rod* was finished it became clear to Lawrence that the idea of " submission to the heroic soul in a greater man" was liable to misinterpretation, in spite of what he had said about leaders and instruments, so he sat down to work out in the relation between Somers and Kangaroo the ideas of false and true leadership, and of false and true friendship. Somers and Kangaroo can never be true friends because Kangaroo wants to feed on Somers' character, to engulf him, and make use of him : he is an incomplete individual looking for something outside himself, or rather an egotist out for an emotional trophy. And just as he can't be a true friend he can't be a true leader, because being unable to offer people the positive attraction of a complete personality, he can only bid for their support by offering them protection from their various anxieties. And as he must have the support of all classes in the community he has to make mutually exclusive and fraudulent bids.

So far, so good. But while Lawrence was coming to this elaboration of his theme, he was also faced with Australian society. Australia has never had a layered society of the English kind, and the traps at the lower end of the social scale—working-class status, lower-middle-class status, and so on, all the things Lawrence was in rebellion against in his personal life—have never existed there. Naturally endowed with conditions leading to the appearance of men and women of fine physical types, the society recognised individuals on the strength of their manhood or womanhood, hardly at all on their social status ; and in return these free individuals submitted to society.

> Hot, big, free-and-easy streets of Sydney : without any sense of an imposition of control. No control, everybody going his own ways with alert harmlessness. On the pavement the foot passengers walked in two divided streams, keeping to the left, and by their unanimity made it impossible for you to wander and look at the shops, if the shops happened to be on your right. . . . And so it was : far more regulated than in London, yet all with a curious voluntariness that oppressed Richard like madness. No control, and no opposition to control. Policemen were cyphers, not noticeable. Every man his own policeman. . . . Yes, the strange unanimity of harmlessness in the crowd had a half paralysing effect on Richard : " Can it be . . . that there is any harm in these people at all ? " They were quick, and their manners were, in a free way, natural and kindly. . . . That was the beauty of the men : their absolute lack of affectation, their naive simplicity, which was at the same time sensitive and gentle. The gentlest country in the world. . . . Who knows what future it may have ? Can a great continent breed a people of this magic harmlessness without becoming a sacrifice of some other, external power ? The land that invites parasites now—where parasites breed like nightmares—what would happen if the power lust came that way ?

Lawrence seems to be suggesting the idea that has recently been worked out in greater detail—and with much greater clarity—by Jung : that an individual or a society in which all conflicts have been resolved is more likely to be dangerous to its neighbours than one in which a conflict of strong and evenly balanced forces exists. There is a need for a conflict and the individual or society unable to meet the need inside will find satisfaction for it outside. But all Lawrence's ideas about the relationships between man and woman and man and man have, up to this point, been based on the conception of an ideal situation in which *fulfilment* or *submission* brings all conflict to an end. *Kangaroo* goes deeply into the nature of the marriage of Richard Somers and his wife Harriet, Lawrence-like and Frieda-like characters, and traces the success of their relationship in the end to the refusal of either to surrender anything of what they are. The marriage is alive because there is no submission about it, both parties have constantly to be reckoned with. Harriet ought theoretically to have submitted to Richard—to " the heroic soul in a greater man " in him, but then the marriage would have been dead. Lawrence in desperation murders Kangaroo abruptly at a political meeting, and runs out of the book, more or less slamming the door behind him :

> I don't love him—I detest him. He can die. I'm glad he is dying. And I don't like Jack either. Not a bit. In fact I like nobody, and there's the end of it, as far as I'm concerned. And if I go round " loving " anybody else, or even " liking " them, I deserve a kick in the guts like Kangaroo.

For the time being Lawrence is purely an anarchist, proposing that relationships should not be anything more than an awareness of difference. His essay on " Democracy," written at about the same time as *Kangaroo*, says :

> When I stand with another man, who is himself, and when I am truly myself, then I am only aware of a presence, and of the strange reality of otherness. There is me, and there is another being . . . there is only this strange recognition of present otherness. . . . And these isolated individuals must be entirely

free. The whole soul of man must never be subjected to motion or emotion, the life activity must never be degra[ded] into a fixed activity, there must be no fixed direction.

Technically *Kangaroo* is a shocking mess, and its sloppy organisation allows one to see clearly all the inherent weakness of Lawrence's working method—or lack of it. But from the various descriptive passages in the book emerges a picture of Australia which has the clarity and power of great poetry ; one sees and feels the storm, and the trip into the bush, at the end of the book just as one sees and feels the opening passages of " The Eve of St. Agnes." Reading *Kangaroo* one feels more acutely than anywhere else the loss that fell when Lawrence turned from seeing and feeling to dogmatising.

Lawrence, however, succeeded—temporarily—in putting the dilemma of *Kangaroo* behind him, and, flying from Australia, recovered his idealism in Mexico ; or, rather, recovered the determination to stick by it in defiance of his knowledge of the truth. *The Plumed Serpent* with enormous pains erects as an ideal the system of relationships mapped out in the two volumes of *The Sisters*—*The Rainbow* and *Women in Love*—and in *Aaron's Rod*. Instead of the awareness of difference between free individuals there is the old ideal of submission, woman to man, and man to greater man ; and this submission purchases between men and women an easy, simple, flowing life dominated by one emotion, and for the men the fixed direction mapped out by their creative leaders. The whole thing is, like *The Woman Who Rode Away*, an outrage, and Lawrence nearly killed himself writing it. Rebellion rears its head in every chapter, and a see-saw battle goes on throughout the book ; whenever Lawrence describes his actual experience of things

Mexican his words betray the theme—in that blighted landscape Ramon and Cipriano could do nothing but found a new parody of some western nationalist power-instrument. Whenever he finds himself engaged in such betrayal Lawrence has to reanimate his ideal with a great mass of words, the camp-meeting revivalist stuff of the hymns of Quetzalcoatl, and the rip-roaring Moody and Sankey preaching that usually follows them as commentary. But however deep the trance induced by word-spinning the reality of the human disaster which is Mexico breaks in again : Lawrence's clear eye is so honest, he cannot fake a vision. He has seen Mexico and, hard as he tries, he cannot distort its reality.

*The Plumed Serpent* is the grave mound of the friendship theme, and the initiation of Cipriano as the Red God Huitzilopotchtli is the last of the curiously embarrassing man-to-man scenes which the theme seems to involve. George and Cyril of *The White Peacock*, farm boys bathing naked in the companionship of work, were the starting-point ; then there was the naked wrestling match between Birkin and Gerald, not by the sweet mill pool but in a stuffy, heavily curtained, heavily carpeted sitting-room, with the furniture pushed back against the walls ; then Lilly oiling Aaron's body, rubbing his lower body and his abdomen with smooth-running oil ; and here in *The Plumed Serpent* :

> . . . then Ramon came quickly to him, placed one of his hands over Cipriano's eyes, closing them. Ramon stood behind Cipriano, who remained motionless in the warm dark, his consciousness reeling in strange concentric waves, towards a centre where it suddenly plunges into the bottomless deeps, like sleep. . . . Then again with a warm, soft pressure, he pressed one naked hand over Cipriano's naked breast, and one between his shoulders. Cipriano stood in profound darkness, erect, and

silent. . . . Ramon . . . put his one hand over the navel, his other hand in the small of the other man's back. . . . Ramon knelt . . . then pressing his head against the hip, folded the arms round Cipriano's loins, closing with his hands the secret places. . . . Then Ramon lifted Cipriano suddenly, with a sleep-moving softness, laid him on the skin of a big mountain lion which was spread upon the blankets . . . and lay down at his feet, holding Cipriano's feet to his own abdomen.

And both men passed into perfect unconsciousness. . . .

Almost certainly when Lawrence first took up this theme he intended to write the curse of homosexuality out of friendship, to free men who felt emotionally drawn to each other in an un-vicious way of the guilt feelings a corrupt society has imposed on such an entirely natural matter. It has to be faced, however, that Lawrence's own sense of guilt makes him desperately uneasy when it comes to this matter. and his own isolation from the world of normal action in which men work together and come to know comradeship and friendship cuts him off from understanding much about its nature. What he drew in *The White Peacock* is the good thing, what he came to draw in *The Plumed Serpent*—this mess of fondling and fainting—is what society—possibly correctly—is afraid of. So far as the friendship theme is concerned *The Plumed Serpent* represents a final failure. Lawrence perhaps recognised it as such, and did not revert to it.

Lawrence also felt that he had failed to make his ideas about the relations between men and women clear : the children of the Morning Star and the daughters of Aphrodite of the foam are manifestly different, but not in any way relevant to life in Wychwood-under-Lyne because the nature of their sexual being is so unhappily complicated with other factors.

Now she understood Ramon's assertion : Man is a column of blood ; woman is a valley of blood . . . now she understood why Ramon and Cipriano wore the white clothes and the sandals, and were naked, or half naked, as living gods. It was the acquiescence in the primitive assertion. It was the renewal of the old terrible bond of the blood-unison of man, which made blood sacrifice so potent a factor of life. The blood of the individual is given back to the great blood being, the god, the nation, the tribe.

It cannot be said that this is in any sense an improvement on the mature Christian conception of human unity in a common being, and it is made even more unattractive by its connection with the idea that there are differently valued grades of the spirit.

And some men are not divine at all. They have only faculties. They are slaves, or they should be slaves.

These men who exist in the blood only, without divinity, must have their leaders—

Ramon was a man, as the least of his peons was a man . . . but only he had that starry power for bringing together the two great human impulses to a point of fusion, for being the bird between the vast wings of the dual-created power to which man has access and in which man has his being. The Morning Star, between the breath of dawn and the deeps of the dark. . . .

And the amorous junketings which end the book are not much help to anyone involved in the normal life of the Midlands.

" Yo !  Yo ! " His eyebrows lifted with queer mock surprise, and a little convulsion went through his body again. " Te quiero mucho ! Mucho te quiero. Mucho ! Mucho ! '

This might be Rudolph Valentino at work. It cannot be much use to anyone faced with real problems, it can only serve in the formation of phantasies, functioning as the Valentino films in providing a temporary escape to a dream world where dream lovers arrive, untrammelled by conventions, from an exotic free zone. When *The Plumed Serpent* was done Lawrence realised that he had, in it, lost himself in that exotic never-never land. While he was still sick and ill he wrote the first chapters of another novel, *The Flying Fish*, which begins with an escape back to the everyday of England from the irrelevant, deadly-for-an-Englishman, exotic of Mexico. But still Gethin Day, the hero of *The Flying Fish*, for all that he is going back to England and English life, is under the domination of a private family Bible written by an Elizabethan ancestor which is more exotic than the campaign literature of *The Plumed Serpent*.

> When earth inert lieth too heavy, then Vesuvius spitteth out fire. And if a nightingale would not sing, his song unsung in him would slay him. For to the nightingale his song is nemesis, and unsung songs are the Erinyes, the impure furies of vengeance. And the sun in thee is thy all in all, so be patient, and take no care. Take no care, for what thou knowest is ever less than what thou art. . . .

Rightly seeing that pseudo-Elizabethan is even less likely to work in the contemporary English mind than Mexican archaism, Lawrence abandoned *The Flying Fish* in the middle of its third chapter, far out in the Atlantic, three days north of Cuba, and still a long way from home.

In *Lady Chatterley's Lover* Lawrence makes his landfall ; Wragby is in the Nottingham coalfield, in the setting of the early short stories. In his last novel Lawrence not only has the advantage of writing about a life he really knows and understands, but he has also reached maturity. The

bogus mysticism has been pruned away, the leadership
theme has vanished, the friendship theme about which he
feels doubt and uncertainty is not brought in to cloud the
main issue : and what is more, the book is written and
constructed so effectively that it is technically the best of
Lawrence's novels.  There are no superfluous characters,
and no inexplicable or irrelevant incidents ; the story flows
along a direct narrative line, action and description are in
perfect balance, and there is little camp-meeting rhetoric.
The only obstacle to the recognition of the book as
Lawrence's best is that it is single-mindedly about sexuality
in its false and true aspects, and that in making clear the
difference between false and true it affronts all the tabus.
Lawrence uses all the Anglo-Saxon monosyllables and discards all Latin polysyllabic technicalities : he writes in
accordance with his belief that sex is a simple, natural thing
for the first time, and, at last, fully achieves the purpose
stated in his letter to A. D. Macleod in 1913.

Lady Chatterley and Mellors, her lover, have explored all
the disappointments and miseries of false sex, of sex poisoned
and made guilty by ideal romantic love, of sex as an
amusement, and of sex as personal satisfaction ; together
they find that their sexual being is part of their essential
state of being and inseparable from all the other parts of
their lives.  Lawrence is widely misinterpreted as saying that
sex is the most important thing in life, and as advocating
promiscuity.  The first part of the message of *Lady Chatterley's
Lover* is a violent attack on promiscuity and the devouring
of a man's being in the flame of sexual irritation, the second
part of the message is the constructive doctrine that man is
whole, mortal flesh and spirit, and that his parts are not at
war with each other.  He cannot come to mental fullness if

he is attempting to repudiate his physical being as a sexual
animal, he cannot know content in the mind if he attempts
to destroy the natural being of his body.  Lawrence has
been accused, too, on the strength of his bad middle period,
of being anti-intellectual.  The charge can be sustained,
Lawrence was anti-intellectual in the sense that Blake was.
He loathed the analytical process that reduces wholes to
elemental fragments, and by revealing the springs of action,
induces paralysis.  Lawrence hated the divisions between
working selves and playing selves, courteous to women in
public selves and dirty-story-telling at the public-house
selves, money-grubbing six-day-a-week selves and Sunday
ideal selves, spiritual selves and bodily selves.  He thought
that the mad destructiveness of our civilisation in our time
was a hysteria induced by these divisions of man's unitary
being, and he attempted to apply, with *Lady Chatterley's
Lover*, the time-honoured cure for hysteria—a shock—a slap
in the face or a douche of cold water.

But slapping a hysteric into calm is not an artistic process,
and like all Lawrence's novels *Lady Chatterley's Lover* is finally
unacceptable as a great work of art, even if the fact is
undeniable that it is the work of a great artist.  The essential
weakness is possibly the importance of agreement ; the
reader who cannot accept Lawrence's ideas cannot admire
the book—it is possible to accept such a real work of art
as *The Idiot*, or *War and Peace*, without accepting all the
beliefs of Dostoewski or Tolstoi.  A secondary weakness is
that *Lady Chatterley's Lover* can only exist during the process
of conversion ; it is a miraculous book while it is bursting
like a bright light on a mind to which the conceptions it
deals with are altogether new, but when the conversion
process is ended the whole thing is so obvious that it seems

Didacticism.

hardly worth saying. To anyone who has achieved a measure of sanity about their physical being it must seem, inevitably, as strange as a novel written to prove that regularity at the stool and a good morning motion are the foundations of mental and physical happiness. It would be an expression of a vital truth, but even though any doctor or district nurse would agree that it might be quite a good thing to have such a novel to bring light to those who darken their lives by giving way to Swift's neurotic feelings on the matter, it would never be treasured as the favourite work of many readers. The end to which Lawrence dedicated his novels was one that was inevitably fatal to him as a novelist.

## CHAPTER IX

EDITH SITWELL accurately enough described Lawrence as the Jaeger poet, and it is difficult to take his
claims to the stature of a poet seriously. He had all
the poet's equipment but he entirely lacked the discipline
that would have allowed him to make use of it. His poems
are notes of image and idea that might be suitable for poetic
expression, but in no case does he get further than the
preliminary draft, the merest hint of what the final poem
might be. Sometimes he prints a group of poems on a
common theme which show this very clearly, they are never
sequences showing an idea in development but they are
alternative solutions to a poetic problem he had not patience
to solve ; the alternatives are set up and the reader can take
his choice. It is difficult when one is reading Lawrence's
poetry not to feel that he looked on it as something easier
than prose—as what sketching is to painting. The anecdote
told by Ada Lawrence about his piano playing is not
altogether irrelevant ; Lawrence sat down to the piano
with quite an amount of theoretical knowledge and the
ability to read music, but he was so angry when he found
that he couldn't just sit down and play like a concert per-
former, that after an hour's struggle he gave up and never
tried to play the piano again. Lawrence takes poetry as far
as you can go without bothering to learn its technique, or
submitting to its mental discipline, as far as you can go by
just wanting to be a poet.

His first volume of poems has an outstanding lack of
merit and among the productions of great men is probably

only equalled in this respect by James Joyce's *Pomes Penyeach*.
Joyce wrote a poem which appears in that collection called
" Alone" which can profitably be compared to Lawrence's early
work :

> The moon's grey-golden meshes make
>   All night a veil,
> The shore lamps on the sleeping lake
>   Laburnum tendrils trail.
>
> The shy reeds whisper to the night
>   A name—her name—
> And all my soul is a delight,
>   A swoon of shame.

In feeling, feebleness of language, and technical ineptness
Joyce's poem is obviously closely allied to this of Lawrence's,
the sixth part of the " Ballad of a Wilful Woman " :

> She gave on the open heather
> Beneath bare judgement stars,
> And she dreamed of her children and Joseph
> And the isles, and her men, and her scars.
>
> And she woke to distil the berries
> The beggar had gathered at night,
> Whence he drew the curious liquors
> He held in delight.
>
> He gave her no crown of flowers,
> No child and no palfrey slow,
> Only led her through harsh hard places
> Where strange winds blow.
>
> She follows the restless wanderings
> Till night when, by the fire's red stain,
> Her face is bent in the bitter steam
> That comes from the flowers of pain.
>
> Then merciless and ruthless
> He takes the flame-wild drops
> To the town, and tries to sell them
> With the market-crops.

> So she follows the cruel journey
> That ends not anywhere,
> And dreams, as she stirs the mixing pot,
> She is brewing hope from despair.

The " flowers of pain "—like Joyce's " swoon of shame "—
sets one immediately on the path through Swinburne to
Rossetti, and in the end to Keats' weaker side—his melan-
choly archaism—and gives one yet another clue to the
essentially Romantic character of Lawrence's thought. The
provincial time-lag, operating in Eastwood as by the Liffey,
introduces an illusory gap between him and Swinburne,
Rossetti and Morris, but he is effectively their immediate
consequence. Rossetti and Swinburne give him the conception of passionate love as the core of life, though he
rejects their obsession with guilt in favour of Morris' sunnier
rationalist views. Morris' Guinevere, passionate, fully
mature, and capable of standing up in the face of Sir
Gawaine and convention to justify her adultery with
Lancelot, is as much the source of Lawrence's central idea
of the good woman as was Frieda. And, poetry apart, there
is hardly an idea of Lawrence's which is not to be found in
Morris' work, the bulk of his political and social conceptions
being found in News From Nowhere.

Edward Marsh showed rare critical acuteness in seeing that
this last swallow from the pre-Raphaelite summer was a
potential poet and tried to make him conscious of the
problems he would have to solve before he could become a
real poet. They corresponded for a period at the end of
1913 ; somewhat in Ruskin's manner Marsh told Lawrence
just why he thought Lawrence's poetry was bad, and
how he could cure its defects. Lawrence replied by argu-
ing away the objections until he became bored with the

correspondence and broke it off in a long letter which shows
just why he never became a poet :

> I only know the verse you quote against me is right, and
> you are wrong. . . . I think I read my poetry more by length
> than by stress—as a matter of movements in space than footsteps
> hitting the earth.

> Just a few of the roses we gathered by the Isar
> Are fallen, and their blood-red petals on the cloth
> Float like boats on a river, waiting
> For a fairy wind to wake them from their sloth.

> I think more of a bird with broad wings flying and lapsing
> through the air, than anything, when I think of metre. . . .
> There is a double method of scanning verse—if you'll notice it.

> I have/forgot much,/Cynara ! / Gone with the/wind,
>     Flung roses,/roses/riotously/with the/throng
> Dancing/to put/thy pale/lost lil/ies out/of mind ;
>     But I/was des/olate,/and sick/of an old/passion. . . .

> Would you scan like that ? I hate an on-foot method of
> reading, I should go :

> I have forgot much, Cynara ! Gone with the wind,
> Flung roses, roses riotously with the throng,
> Dancing to put thy pale, lost, lilies out of mind ;
>     But I was desolate, and sick of an old passion. . . .

It all depends on the pause—the natural pause, the natural
lingering of the voice according to the feeling—it is the hidden
emotional pattern that makes poetry, not the obvious form.
. . . It is the lapse of the feeling, something as indefinite as
expression in the voice carrying emotion. It doesn't depend
on the ear, particularly, but on the sensitive soul. And the ear
gets a habit, and becomes master, when the ebbing and lifting
emotion should be master, and the ear the transmitter. If your
ear has got stiff and mechanical, don't blame my poetry. . . .

I don't write for your ear. That is the constant war, I reckon, between new expression and the habituated, mechanical trans-mitters and receivers of the human constitution. . . . I can't tell you what pattern I see in any poetry, save one complete thing. . . . I always wonder if the Greeks and Romans really did scan, or if scansion wasn't a thing invented afterwards by the schoolmaster. Yet I seem to find the same number of long lingering notes in each line. I know nothing about it, I only know you aren't right. . . . Don't talk to me any more about poetry for months—unless it's other men's work. I really love verse, even rubbish. But I'm fearfully busy at a novel, and brush all the gossamer of verse off my face.

It is of passing interest to notice that the verse of his own Lawrence quotes in that letter was revised before it was printed in *Look ! We Have Come Through !*

> Just a few of the roses we gathered from the Isar
> Are fallen, and their mauve-red petals on the cloth
> Float like boats on a river, while other
> Roses are ready to fall, reluctant and loth.

The changes are not really motivated by poetic considera-tions ; the shop-soiled *blood-red* has been changed because Lawrence has noticed the blueish tinge which empurples red rose petals when the flowers become overblown and he wants to be more accurate—but *mauve-red* is a contradiction, made of two opposed parts. The changes of the second and third lines are motivated by an attempt to dodge Marsh's suggestion that it is nonsense to talk of waking someone from sloth, which is a waking state : they are also a deliberate piece of perversity ; Marsh had objected to cloth-sloth as a bogus rhyme, a low-class optical booby trap, and Lawrence endows the roses with will and consciousness just as much to save that false rhyme as to save the sense.

What Lawrence achieves in poetry is indistinguishable from the effects he achieves in the flowing passages of his prose, written when he was in a state of excitement. It is really the fixing of rhetoric chanted to the inner ear. The inner ear is not over-critical, as the poems which one writes in dreams bear witness, and in its fondness for an even flow will let details slide. The passage quoted on page 87 from *The Man Who Loved Islands* based on the sounds from the phrase " the days were beginning to lengthen " is typical of Lawrence's poetry : like the rest of it, it answers if the reader gives himself up to the flow and shares Lawrence's excitement, and fails if the reader remains detached and critical of detail. Every poet knows this initial act of creation for the excitable and uncritical inner listener, and good poets, aware that it is an initial act, recognise it as the beginning of a long and arduous creative process. Lawrence's poems remain in the initial stage, drafts, notes for the later stages, and his books of verse are notebooks for something unachieved. Sometimes, as in *Birds, Beasts and Flowers*, achievement is very close, but there is always the carelessness of the cloth-sloth rhyme to spoil even his best poetry :

> Dawn-rose
> Sub-delighted, stone-engendered,
> Cyclamens, young cyclamens
> Arching
> Waking, pricking their ears
> Like delicate very-young greyhound bitches
> Half-yawning at the open, inexperienced
> Vista of day,
> Folding back their soundless petalled ears
>
> Greyhound bitches
> Sending their rosy muzzled pensive down,
> And breathing soft, unwilling to wake to the new day
> Yet sub-delighted.

The poem, " Sicilian Cyclamens," is as a whole delightful, one of Lawrence's loveliest lyrics ; it might have survived *sub-delighted* once, it cannot survive the second use. It is apparent in the whole body of Lawrence's writing that he has a sensitive ear and that he recognises the real value of such a word, or rather compound, as *sub-delighted* ; when such words appear they do not represent lapses. Like the change *sloth* to *loth*, they represent deliberate attempts to be uncouth—they are on a footing with Mellors' reversions to dialect in *Lady Chatterley's Lover*. When Mellors is at his self-conscious worst trying to affront the people who possess the trimmings of social superiority he drops into coarse speech to affront them ; Lawrence is at his self-conscious worst faced with the cultural elaborations surrounding the craft of poetry and is then at pains to be every inch the rough diamond from the Nottingham coalfield ; in the end his poetic self is as fraudulent a phantom as the mole-skinned stage rustic created by Housman to be responsible for his poetry.

The ideas expressed in the poems can generally be found elsewhere in Lawrence's work, poem and prose being closely related in the manner discussed above in the case of the two pieces of prose—*A Letter from Germany* and *The Border Line*. Sometimes one can see in his letters the immediate recording of an experience which later becomes a poem, as in his letters from Ceylon one finds the bones of the poem " Elephant," from *Birds, Beasts and Flowers*. Generally the development is from prose to fuller expression in poetry when it is concerned with matters of experience, but the development sometimes takes place in the other direction when it is a question of ideas. The ideas expressed in *Love Poems and Others, Amores*, and *Look ! We Have Come*

*Through !* about the nature of the emotions uniting men and women, or dividing them, are fragments of the *Study of Thomas Hardy*, which is in a sense the final draft of the poems. It is also clear that the later poems and *Pansies* are fragments of a number of complete works, the essays, " Education of the People," " Reality of Peace " and " Democracy," and condensations of parts of the novels ; but the development is consistently towards the final poem. The three poems in *Last Poems* called " Self-sacrifice," "Shedding of Blood " and " The Old Idea of Sacrifice " have their origin in Chapter XIV of *Kangaroo*, are carried on a stage in Chapter XXVI of *The Plumed Serpent*, and reach their final shape at Bandol in 1928–9. The whole process thus covers five or six years.

Towards the end of his life Lawrence's opinion of poetry was changing ; when he began he compared it—

> to the droppings of goats among the rocks, mere excreta that fertilises the ground it falls on.

then he admitted the importance of the novel—

> ⋅ Nothing is important but life . . . the novel is the book of life. Books are not life. They are only tremulations of the ether. But the novel as a tremulation can make the whole man alive tremble. Which is more than poetry, philosophy, science or any other book-tremulation can do.

and finally he conceded poetry a place of equal importance to the whole man alive—

> the essential quality of poetry is that it makes a new effort of attention, and discovers a new world within the known world.

A function which he considered to be a vital one, the known

world being always a comforting falsehood and the poet's new world being reality. But he discovered this truth too late to make the discovery of new worlds, too late to make his poetry more than a sometimes dazzling display of his own personality.

CHAPTER X

IT is probably a mistake to treat Lawrence as a literary
man when one attempts to assess his place in his time : he
belongs not with those who were primarily writers and
artists, but with those who were livers and life-changers,
and writers more or less incidentally. He is closer to Ruskin
and William Morris than to anyone else of recent times,
with his highly personal bias and nervous irritability nearer
Ruskin than Morris. He is closer to Ruskin, too, in that
his lack of worldliness made his political statements as
impassioned as a statement of religious belief, where Morris
could see and adjust his speech to the necessities of municipal
ward politics. Lawrence is very like Ruskin, too, in his
rapid transitions from the hardest commonsense to the
sublimest sun-luminous mountain mist, and in his readiness
to utter the final truth on any matter at the drop of a hat.
*Psychoanalysis and the Unconscious* (1921) and *Fantasia of the
Unconscious* (1922) strengthen this comparison, although
psychoanalysis is a subject which one cannot readily consider
in connection with Ruskin ; what is Ruskinian in Lawrence
in this connection is the megalomaniac self-confidence which
allowed him to write them at all. Lawrence knew virtually
nothing of psychoanalysis when he wrote the two books,
just as Ruskin knew virtually nothing of economics when
he plunged into conflict with the economists of his day,
and but precious little geology when he plunged against the
theorists of glacial erosion. But nothing could stop either
man when he knew that he was right ; any marshalling of
facts in opposition was quite useless, both men could dispose

of any evidence against them by the simple process of saying, " I know the truth behind your facts and I can tell you that you are concerned with illusions." Men who argue in such a fashion are difficult to catch out on the practical level, there is nothing to get hold of, and the only defence is abuse ; Ruskin and Lawrence were abused in much the same terms by much the same sort of people. But in the long run, when the heat of the argument has died down, it is just as difficult to be precise in deciding what good they have done. Their influence has been great, but just what their influence has brought about it would be difficult to say—it is diffused in the general state of our being. Ruskin did force a general recognition of the vital importance of justice and humane principle in any economic system, and every elementary school in the kingdom to-day puts his doctrine that art is an essential part of life into rudimentary practice. The route by which individuals to-day come to reject the injustice and inhumanity of Communism or Fascism is not, however, immediately apparent, and that it leads back to Ruskin and *Fors Clavigera* is not obvious ; nor are the art teachers in elementary schools consciously Ruskinians. The ideas themselves, moreover, are not original with Ruskin, but it was he who injected them into the popular stream of ideas and brought them from the realm of advanced theory into the public domain. It is the same with Lawrence ; the details of his actual doctrines are blurred and rubbed with usage, partially forgotten, but their vital parts contribute to the living faith of an immense number of people, people who are none the less Lawrentine for not knowing it. Everyone who, worried by an abnormality of their own or their children's sexual behaviour, treats the thing not as a secret shame but a problem to be discussed frankly with a doctor or psychiatrist is under the influence of Lawrence. It may not be Lawrence who gave them the idea, they may have had it from the home page of a daily newspaper, or from a talk on the wireless, but it was largely because Lawrence spread his doctrines in his time that they are discussed at that level in ours. Beyond doubt the sexual behaviour of most literate people who married or reached puberty after 1925 has been profoundly affected by his writing, and beyond doubt his influence in that direction has been mainly good. For every single reader who has found in his work the justification of libertinism there must be dozens who have read more intelligently to find Lawrence a help in dispelling fears and apprehensions, and in making their sexual being the crowning enrichment of their emotional lives, instead of its shameful or sordid appendage.

> I can only write what I feel pretty strongly about : and that, at present, is the relation between men and women. After all, it is the problem of to-day, the establishment of a new relation, or the readjustment of the old one, between men and women.

His dream of Rananim may have been absurd, he may have failed to win immortality as an artist, but he succeeded in the purpose to which he dedicated himself at the beginning of his career.

1911. *The White Peacock* (a novel).

1912. *The Trespasser* (a novel).

1913. *Sons and Lovers* (a novel).
*Love Poems and Others* (poetry).

1914. *The Prussian Officer* (short stories).
*The Widowing of Mrs. Holroyd* (a play).

1915. *The Rainbow* (a novel).

1916. *Amores* (poetry).
*Twilight in Italy* (descriptive essays).

1917. *Look ! We Have Come Through !* (poetry).

1918. *New Poems* (poetry).

1919. *Bay* (poetry).

1920. *Women in Love* (a novel).
*The Lost Girl* (a novel).
*Touch and Go* (a play).

1921. *Psychoanalysis and the Unconscious* (an essay).
*Sea and Sardinia* (descriptive essays).
*Movements in European History* (an historical study).

1922. *Aaron's Rod* (a novel).
*England, My England* (short stories).
*Tortoises* (poetry).

1923. *Kangaroo* (a novel).
*The Ladybird* (short stories).
*Birds, Beasts and Flowers* (poetry).
*Fantasia of the Unconscious* (an essay).
*Studies in Classical American Literature* (criticism).
(A translation of Giovanni Verga's *Mastro don Gesualdo*.)

1924. *The Boy in the Bush* (a novel in collaboration with Miss M. L. Skinner).

1925. *St. Mawr* and *The Princess* (short stories).
*Reflections on the Death of a Porcupine* (essays).
(A translation, Giovanni Verga's *Little Novels of Sicily*.)

1926. *The Plumed Serpent* (a novel).
  *Sun* (a short story).
  *Glad Ghosts* (a short story).
  *David* (a play).
1927. *Mornings in Mexico* (descriptive essays).
1928. *Lady Chatterley's Lover* (a novel).
  *Rawdon's Roof* (short story).
  *The Woman Who Rode Away* (short stories).
  *Collected Poems* (for which many early poems were almost entirely rewritten).
  (A translation, Giovanni Verga's *Cavalleria Rusticana*.)
1929. *The Escaped Cock* (short story, renamed and republished as *The Man Who Died*).
  *Pansies* (poetry).
  *Pornography and Obscenity* (an essay).
  *The Paintings of D. H. Lawrence* (reproductions of the pictures exhibited at the Warren Galleries, with a preface by Lawrence).
  (A translation, A. F. Grazzini's *The Story of Dr. Manente*).
1930. *The Virgin and the Gipsy* (a short novel).
  *Love Among the Haystacks* (short stories). (The title story of this volume, and "Once," the last story in it, are not included in the Heinemann omnibus volume of short stories.)
  *Nettles* (poetry).
  *The Triumph of the Machine* (a poem).
  *A propos of "Lady Chatterley's Lover"* (an essay).
1931. *The Man Who Died* (short story).
  *Apocalypse* (an essay).
1932. *Etruscan Places* (descriptive essays, unfinished).

A number of Lawrence's most important essays, either unpublished or obscurely published at the time of his death, were collected and published under the title of *Phœnix* by Messrs. Heinemann, in 1936. The volume, which includes his essays on "Education," "The Reality of Peace," and "Democracy" and his "Study of Thomas Hardy," is one of four uniform volumes : *The Letters of D. H. Lawrence*, which has a preface by Aldous Huxley ; *The Tales of D. H. Lawrence*, which includes forty-seven of his short stories, but unhappily omits "Love Among the Haystacks" and "Once" ; and *The Collected Poems of D. H. Lawrence*.